How to Use
MICROSOFT
WORKS

How to Use
MICROSOFT
WORKS

BRUCE GENDRON

Illustrated by
DAVE FEASEY AND L.J. BLAKE

Ziff-Davis Press
Emeryville, California

Copy Editor	Jan Jue
Technical Reviewer	Heidi Steele
Project Coordinator	Barbara Dahl
Proofreader	Carol Burbo
Cover Illustration	Regan Honda
Cover Design	Carrie English and Regan Honda
Book Design	Dennis Gallagher/Visual Strategies, San Francisco
Screen Graphics Editor	Cat Haglund
Technical Illustration	Dave Feasey and L.J. Blake
Word Processing	Howard Blechman
Page Layout	Bruce Lundquist
Indexer	Carol Burbo

Ziff-Davis Press books are produced on a Macintosh computer system with the following applications: FrameMaker®, Microsoft® Word, QuarkXPress®, Adobe Illustrator®, Adobe Photoshop®, Adobe Streamline™, MacLink® *Plus*, Aldus® FreeHand™, Collage Plus™.

If you have comments or questions or would like to receive a free catalog, call or write:
Ziff-Davis Press
5903 Christie Avenue
Emeryville, CA 94608
1-800-688-0448

ISBN 1-56276-214-1

Manufactured in the United States of America
❁ This book is printed on paper that contains 50% total recycled fiber of which 20% is de-inked postconsumer fiber.
10 9 8 7 6 5 4

To my parents

TABLE OF CONTENTS

To get the most out of this book, read it in sequence. If you have any experience with Microsoft Windows or Microsoft Works, you may already be familiar with the information in some of the chapters. However, skimming those chapters will provide a useful refresher on major concepts and terminology.

Welcome aboard.

CHAPTER 1

What Is Microsoft Works?

 Microsoft Works is a software package that helps you do many of the most popular and important tasks you can perform on your computer.

Microsoft Works, or just plain "Works," is an *integrated software* package. It combines the features of the most widely used software packages into a neat and easy-to-use bundle.

The part most people want to use first is the *word processor.* A word processor is software that helps you create documents. A document is simply anything written. It can be the Declaration of Independence, your shopping list, or anything in between.

The second part is a spreadsheet, which is a tool to help you perform and record mathematical calculations. You might use it to calculate your company's quarterly earnings, your personal budget, or even the returns you'll receive from the investment of your lottery winnings.

The third part is a powerful electronic database. A database is any collection of information. Mailing lists, Rolodexes, and compilations of baseball players' statistics are all databases.

The fourth part, and the last one we'll cover in this book, is a communications program for exchanging information with other computers.

Separately, these programs help you accomplish all of the basic computer tasks. Together in Microsoft Works, they form one of the most powerful and versatile software packages around.

How to Put Microsoft Works to Work

Microsoft Works holds an unusual position in the world of software. Its true power lies not in any one of its parts, but in the ease with which you can combine them to fit your needs. Here are just a few simple examples of what Microsoft Works can do for you.

1 With just a little experience, you'll discover that word processors can be the easiest way of creating documents. Word processors let you do your own writing, formatting, editing, revising, and printing without ever leaving your chair.

5 Connecting PCs to bulletin boards and information services is becoming a very popular and important means of communication. The communications feature in Microsoft Works lets even a computer novice get started easily.

4 With the help of the database and the word processor, you can create personalized letters to a large number of people.

TIP SHEET

▶ **This book is about version 3.0 of Microsoft Works. If you don't have version 3.0, some of the material in this book may not apply to you. Check your Microsoft Works packaging or documentation if you're not sure.**

▶ **Chapter 2 of this book is for first-time computer or Windows users. If you can start Microsoft Windows, use the mouse, choose commands from a menu, and make selections in a dialog box, skip ahead to Chapter 3. If you can't do all of these things (or if you don't even know what they mean!), Chapter 2 is just for you.**

2 Spreadsheets are useful for performing calculations. The more numbers you have to manipulate, or the more repetition in your calculations, the greater the benefit.

3 The most popular use of databases is to keep mailing lists, but they can help you organize any information.

Personal information from database

Font: Times New Roman, Size: 12 points

Boldface

Left-aligned text

Labels mixed with numbers

Flawless line breaks

Italics

Justified text

Center-aligned text

Table from spreadsheet

Numerical calculations

Right-aligned numbers

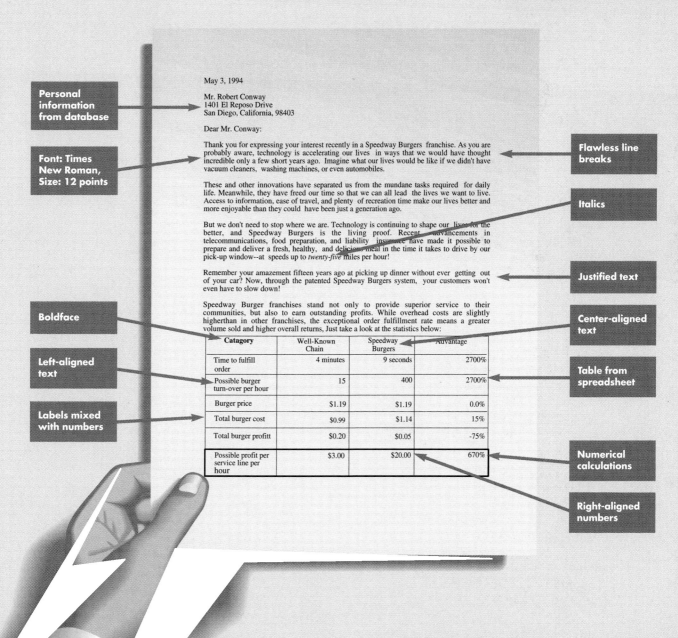

May 3, 1994

Mr. Robert Conway
1401 El Reposo Drive
San Diego, California, 98403

Dear Mr. Conway:

Thank you for expressing your interest recently in a Speedway Burgers franchise. As you are probably aware, technology is accelerating our lives in ways that we would have thought incredible only a few short years ago. Imagine what our lives would be like if we didn't have vacuum cleaners, washing machines, or even automobiles.

These and other innovations have separated us from the mundane tasks required for daily life. Meanwhile, they have freed our time so that we can all lead the lives we want to live. Access to information, ease of travel, and plenty of recreation time make our lives better and more enjoyable than they could have been just a generation ago.

But we don't need to stop where we are. Technology is continuing to shape our lives for the better, and Speedway Burgers is the living proof. Recent advancements in telecommunications, food preparation, and liability insurance have made it possible to prepare and deliver a fresh, healthy, and delicious meal in the time it takes to drive by our pick-up window--at speeds up to *twenty-five* miles per hour!

Remember your amazement fifteen years ago at picking up dinner without ever getting out of your car? Now, through the patented Speedway Burgers system, your customers won't even have to slow down!

Speedway Burger franchises stand not only to provide superior service to their communities, but also to earn outstanding profits. While overhead costs are slightly higher than in other franchises, the exceptional order fulfillment rate means a greater volume sold and higher overall returns, Just take a look at the statistics below:

Catagory	Well-Known Chain	Speedway Burgers	Advantage
Time to fulfill order	4 minutes	9 seconds	2700%
Possible burger turn-over per hour	15	400	2700%
Burger price	$1.19	$1.19	0.0%
Total burger cost	$0.99	$1.14	15%
Total burger profitt	$0.20	$0.05	-75%
Possible profit per service line per hour	$3.00	$20.00	670%

CHAPTER 2

What Are DOS and Windows?

 DOS and Windows are programs that enable you to run all the programs you really want to run: your database, your communications program—all of which are included in Microsoft Works—your games, and so on.

DOS, short for *disk operating system*, copies information to and from the disks in your computer. Without an operating system, your computer cannot do anything useful for you. You cannot run a program like Microsoft Works unless you tell DOS to copy it temporarily from the disk into *random-access memory (RAM)*, a temporary holding place. Likewise, you cannot electronically store and later reuse a document unless you have DOS copy it from RAM onto a disk.

Windows can simplify your role in directing these and many other affairs on your computer. It also provides a consistent and fairly appealing backdrop for Windows-based programs such as Microsoft Works. Windows-based programs look comfortingly similar on the screen, and there are many similarities in the ways you work with them. If you've used any Windows-based program, certain Microsoft Works operations will be familiar to you.

You don't need to "start" DOS. It is running whenever you are using your computer. Windows, on the other hand, is an add-on program that may or may not be running as you use your computer. But Windows *must* be running before you can use Microsoft Works or any other Windows-based program. This chapter helps you start and run Windows.

How to Start Windows from DOS

The heart and soul of DOS, at least from the user's viewpoint, is the *DOS prompt*. This is where DOS asks you for information and you provide it. By typing *commands* at the DOS prompt, you can run programs, check the contents of your disks, reset the time on your computer's internal clock, and much more. For now, the only DOS command you absolutely must know is the one to start Windows.

TIP SHEET

▶ **Your computer may be set up to bypass the DOS prompt and start Windows automatically. If Windows has started, you'll see the words *Program Manager* somewhere on the screen. In this case, you can skip steps 4 and 5—whose purpose is, after all, to help you start Windows.**

▶ **Some computers automatically run the *DOS Shell,* a program designed to improve the DOS interface, upon start-up. If your computer is running the DOS Shell, you'll see the words *MS-DOS Shell* across the top of the screen. Hold down the Alt key as you type fx to exit the DOS Shell and face the DOS prompt. Then proceed with step 4.**

▶ **Your office computer specialist may have set up a *custom menu* that appears in place of the DOS prompt. This menu should contain an entry for *Windows* (or possibly *Microsoft Windows* or *Windows 3.1* or a similar variation). To start Windows, you probably have to press the ↓ key until the Windows entry is highlighted, and then press Enter. However, you may have to consult with your office computer specialist to learn how the custom menu works.**

1 Switch on your computer. You may need to flick switches on several components of your computer system, including the main box containing the hard disk and the floppy-disk drives, the monitor (screen), and the printer. Give the computer a minute or so to go through its wake-up ritual. When it's ready to accept information from you, it will ask you for the information or display the DOS prompt.

2 Provide any information the computer asks for, and press the
Enter key when done. Some computers ask for the date and time.
If your computer is on a *network*—a setup where personal computers in an office are hooked together to share information—it
may ask you for your name and password. (Your office's network
administrator can help you with this step.)

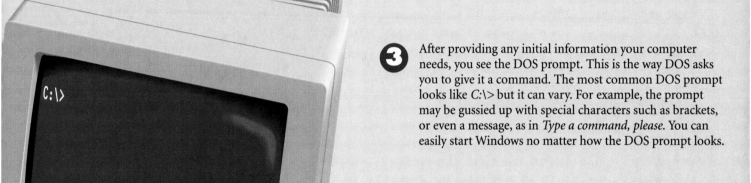

3 After providing any initial information your computer
needs, you see the DOS prompt. This is the way DOS asks
you to give it a command. The most common DOS prompt
looks like *C:\>* but it can vary. For example, the prompt
may be gussied up with special characters such as brackets,
or even a message, as in *Type a command, please.* You can
easily start Windows no matter how the DOS prompt looks.

4 Type **win** and press the Enter key. On most computers,
this command starts Windows. After a few seconds, you'll
see *Program Manager* somewhere on the screen, indicating
that Windows is now running. Skip the next step if this
step worked fine.

5 If the preceding step produced a message such as *Bad command or file name*,
try typing **c:\windows\win** and pressing Enter. If that fails, try **d:\windows\win**.
Still can't start Windows? Well, the possible reasons and solutions are too many
to enumerate here, but a computer-savvy colleague should be able to help you
in short order. Or call Microsoft technical support, which fields questions like
yours routinely.

How to Start a Program from Program Manager

Program Manager is a Windows-based program that comes with Windows. Its role is to make it easy to start *other* programs, including Microsoft Works. Program Manager opens when you start Windows and remains open as long as Windows is running. This picture shows how Program Manager might look when you start Windows. Then again, Windows is highly customizable, so your starting screen could look quite different.

TIP SHEET

▶ To open a *program group* window using the keyboard, press the Alt key, type w to pull down the Window menu, and type the number next to the program group you want to open. To start a program using the keyboard, open its program group window, use the arrow keys to highlight the name of the program, and press Enter.

▶ Under Windows, you can have more than one program running at a time. After starting one program, press Alt+Esc (hold down Alt, press and release Esc, and release Alt) to return to Program Manager. Then find and start the next program. Use the Alt+Esc key combination to switch among all your open programs.

▶ To close a document window, double-click on the *Control Menu* box in its upper-left corner. You can close an application window the same way. This has the effect of shutting down the program. Closing the Program Manager application window closes Windows and returns you to the DOS prompt (or to a custom menu or DOS Shell if one of these programs was running when you started Windows).

1 A *window* is simply an on-screen box containing information. Like most Windows-based programs, Program Manager has an *application window* and multiple *document windows*. In this screen, six windows are wholly or partially visible. Solitaire, Microsoft Works, Calculator, and Program Manager are application windows. HOLIDAY.WPS and Accessories are document windows.

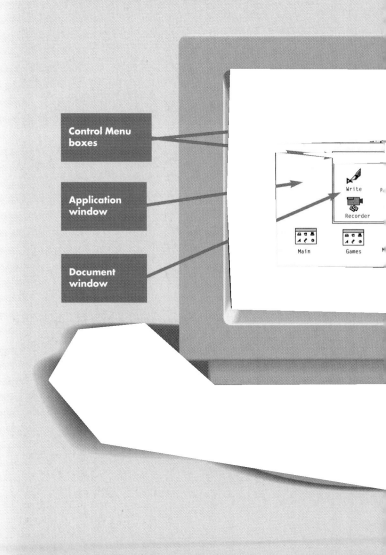

Control Menu boxes

Application window

Document window

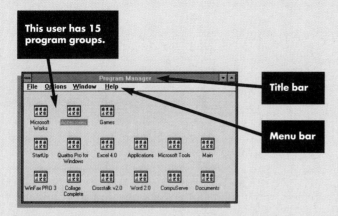

This user has 15 program groups.

Title bar

Menu bar

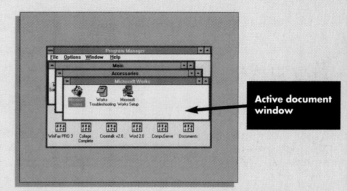

Active document window

2 An application window contains a *title bar,* which displays the program name—in this case, Program Manager. You issue commands from a program's *menu bar.* The application window for Program Manager also contains icons representing *program groups,* collections of related programs that you can run.

3 There can be zero, one, or multiple document windows open at one time, but only one document window is *active.* The active document window is the one that will be affected by commands you issue. The title bar of each document window contains the document name, and the title bar of the active document window is highlighted.

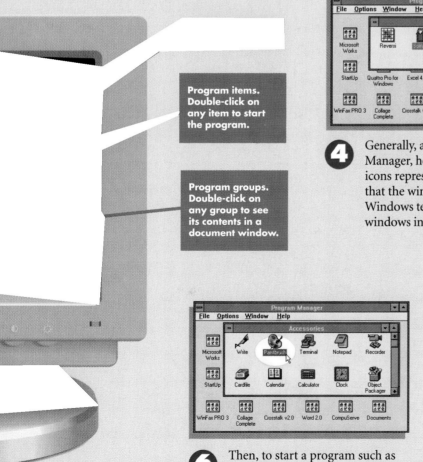

Program items. Double-click on any item to start the program.

Program groups. Double-click on any group to see its contents in a document window.

The Games document window contains three program items.

4 Generally, a document window contains a document. In Program Manager, however, document windows contain *program items,* little icons representing the programs within a program group. The fact that the window is called a "document window" is a quirk of Windows terminology. For clarity, many people refer to document windows in Program Manager as *program group windows.*

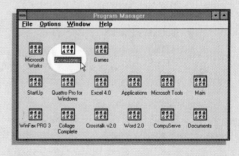

6 Then, to start a program such as Paintbrush, locate its program item in the program group window, roll the mouse to point to the program name or icon, and double-click.

5 When you want to start a program, first open the program group containing its program item. To open a program group such as Accessories, roll the mouse until the arrow points to the group name or icon, and then click the left mouse button twice in rapid succession ("double-click").

How to Use the Mouse in Windows

An *input device* is a means of giving instructions to the computer. You're probably familiar with the keyboard as the most common input device. A *mouse,* so named for its hunched-over appearance and tail-like cable, is a hand-held input device that, along with the keyboard, is one of the two input devices most people use routinely in Windows. Although it's possible to get by without a mouse and do all your work from the keyboard, it's not too wise. The Windows interface was designed with the mouse in mind. Keyboard alternatives can be awkward—and it's not always easy to find out what they are. Take a few minutes to learn the major mouse moves, and you'll be rewarded with smoother computing.

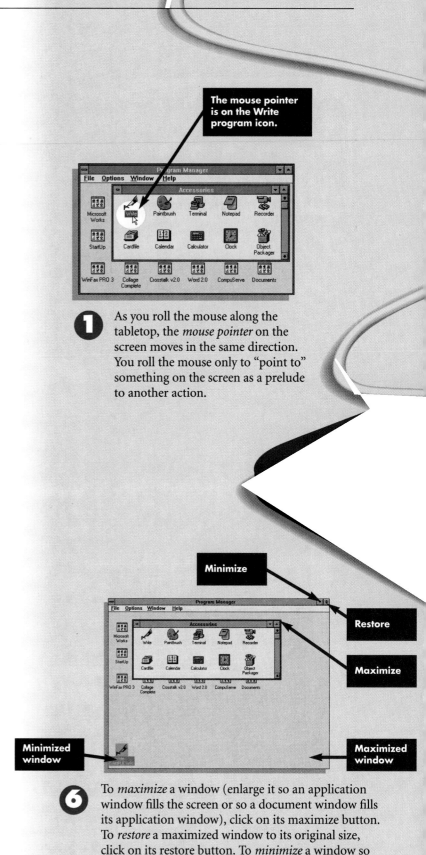

The mouse pointer is on the Write program icon.

1 As you roll the mouse along the tabletop, the *mouse pointer* on the screen moves in the same direction. You roll the mouse only to "point to" something on the screen as a prelude to another action.

Minimize

Restore

Maximize

Minimized window

Maximized window

6 To *maximize* a window (enlarge it so an application window fills the screen or so a document window fills its application window), click on its maximize button. To *restore* a maximized window to its original size, click on its restore button. To *minimize* a window so it's merely an icon with a title, click on its minimize button. To restore a minimized window to its original size, double-click on its title or icon.

TIP SHEET

▶ Unless told otherwise, use the *left* mouse button. The other mouse buttons are used so infrequently in Windows that when they are used, you're always told about it specifically.

▶ Some mice have two buttons, and others have three. The right mouse button is used infrequently, and the middle button on the three-button mouse is almost never used.

▶ For keyboard alternatives to the scroll bars and the maximize/minimize/restore buttons, turn the page.

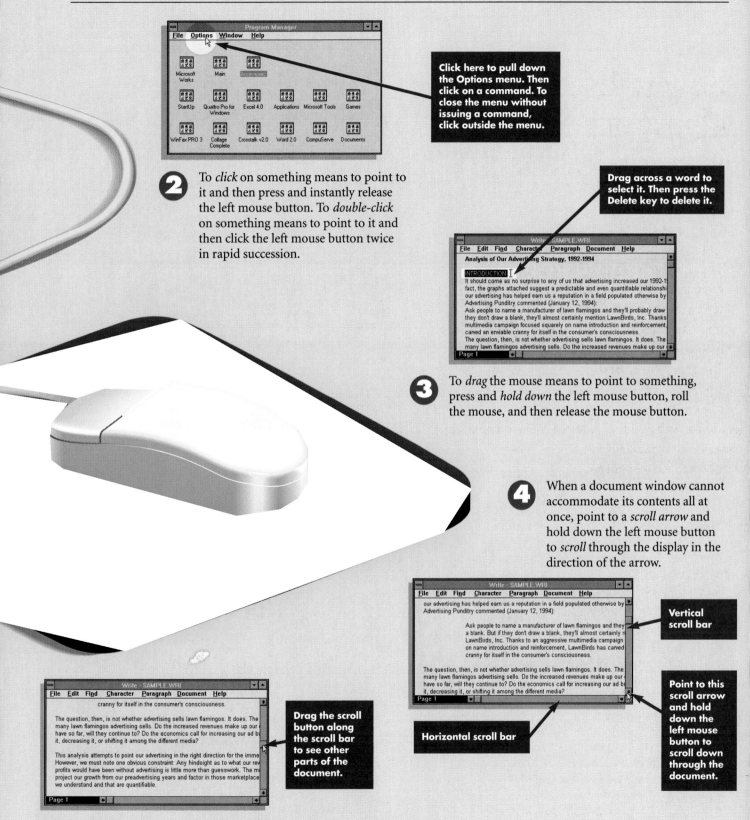

Click here to pull down the Options menu. Then click on a command. To close the menu without issuing a command, click outside the menu.

2 To *click* on something means to point to it and then press and instantly release the left mouse button. To *double-click* on something means to point to it and then click the left mouse button twice in rapid succession.

Drag across a word to select it. Then press the Delete key to delete it.

3 To *drag* the mouse means to point to something, press and *hold down* the left mouse button, roll the mouse, and then release the mouse button.

4 When a document window cannot accommodate its contents all at once, point to a *scroll arrow* and hold down the left mouse button to *scroll* through the display in the direction of the arrow.

Vertical scroll bar

Point to this scroll arrow and hold down the left mouse button to scroll down through the document.

Drag the scroll button along the scroll bar to see other parts of the document.

Horizontal scroll bar

5 Another way to scroll is to drag the scroll button to a new location on the scroll bar. The position of the scroll button suggests what part of the contents you are viewing. For example, when the scroll button is about one-third of the way down the vertical scroll bar in a document window, you are one-third of the way from the top of the document.

How to Use the Keyboard in Windows

In Windows and in most Windows-based programs, you don't have to use the keyboard for much of anything—except, of course, to type text. But if you type quite a bit, you may be interested in optional ways to move through documents, issue commands, and perform other common actions without having to reach for the mouse. The more experience you get in a Windows-based program, the more likely you'll hanker for keyboard alternatives to the mouse actions you perform most often. Even if you're a true mouse-o-phile, you should be aware of the major keyboard techniques in case your mouse ever malfunctions.

1 The Shift, Alt, and Ctrl keys always work in combination with other keys. No doubt you know that pressing the Shift key along with a letter key types a capital letter. The other available combinations vary by program.

6 Not surprisingly, the Escape key (Esc on most keyboards) lets you slam the door on possible hazards. If you pull down a menu but decide not to issue a command, press Esc twice to deactivate the menu bar. If you issue a command and a dialog box appears (see next page) but you don't want to proceed, press Esc to close the dialog box.

TIP SHEET

▶ In many programs, the PgUp and PgDn keys scroll the window contents in large increments, Ctrl+Home moves to the top of the window contents, and Ctrl+End moves to the bottom.

▶ Your function keys may be across the top of the keyboard or along the left side. Function keys along the side are easier for touch typists to reach and may make it worthwhile to memorize some keyboard shortcuts in your favorite programs.

2 Most often, Shift, Alt, and Ctrl combine with the *function keys*—labeled F1 through F10 or F12—as an alternative way to issue a command. For example, in most Windows programs, press Alt+F4 (hold down Alt, press and release F4, and release Alt) to close the program. The function keys can also work alone.

3 When you don't want to reach for the mouse to scroll through the contents of a window, use the ↑, ↓, ←, and → keys instead. If the arrows on the numeric keypad don't work, press the Num Lock key and they should work fine.

Control menu of the Accessories document window

4 To maximize, minimize, restore, or close a window, first open its Control menu. Press Alt+spacebar to open the Control menu of an application window; press Alt+hyphen to open the Control menu of a document window. Use the ↓ key to highlight the command you want: Maximize, Minimize, Restore, or Close. Then press Enter.

Type the underlined character to issue the command.

5 To pull down a menu from the menu bar, press Alt and then type the underlined character in the menu name. Then, to issue a command from the menu, type the underlined character in the command name.

How to Talk to a Dialog Box

A *dialog box* is where you give Windows (or a Windows-based program) the information it needs to carry out a command you have issued. Say you issue a command called Print, a command found in many programs. Before doing any printing, the program may present a dialog box to ask you how much of the window contents to print, how many copies to print, what printer to print it on, and so forth. Once you answer, the Print command takes effect. The name *dialog box* is just slightly misleading. In a human dialog, the participants take turns speaking. In a computerized dialog, the program asks all its questions at once, and then you give all your answers. It's more like a questionnaire than a dialog.

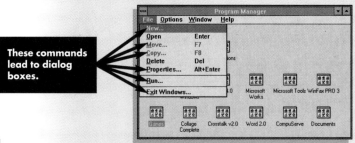

These commands lead to dialog boxes.

1 In Windows menus, the presence of three dots after a command name means that a dialog box will appear when you issue the command.

6 When you've provided all the information requested, issue the command by clicking on the button labeled OK or on another appropriately named button. (The button name might be Print or Find or something else related to the command.)

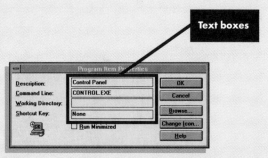

Text boxes

5 To change the entry in a *text box*, first click anywhere in the box. Then use the arrow keys to position the cursor, use the Backspace and Delete keys to delete text as needed, and type new text from the keyboard.

TIP SHEET

▶ **To choose a dialog box option from the keyboard, hold down Alt and type the underlined character in the option name. If the dialog box lacks underlined characters, press Tab to move from option to option. Then, to mark or clear a check box, press the spacebar. To mark the desired radio button within a group, use the arrow keys. To drop down a list, press the down arrow key; then press the down arrow to highlight your choice, and press Tab. To edit the contents of a text box, use the arrow keys, Backspace, Delete, and ordinary typing keys.**

▶ **If you need to see what's behind a dialog box, move the box by dragging its title bar.**

▶ **To close a dialog box without issuing the command, click on the Cancel button (available in most dialog boxes), double-click on the box's Control Menu box, or press Esc.**

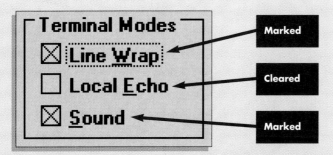

Marked

Cleared

Marked

2 One way to answer a question in a dialog box is to mark or clear a square *check box*. Click in an empty check box to mark it, accepting the option; click in a marked check box to clear it and reject the option.

3 Sometimes options are grouped in *radio buttons*. You can select only one option at a time in the group. Select an option by clicking in the round button; the previously selected button is cleared. It's just like the station-selector buttons on old-time car radios—hence the name.

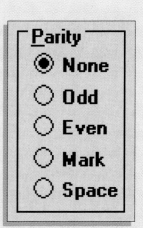

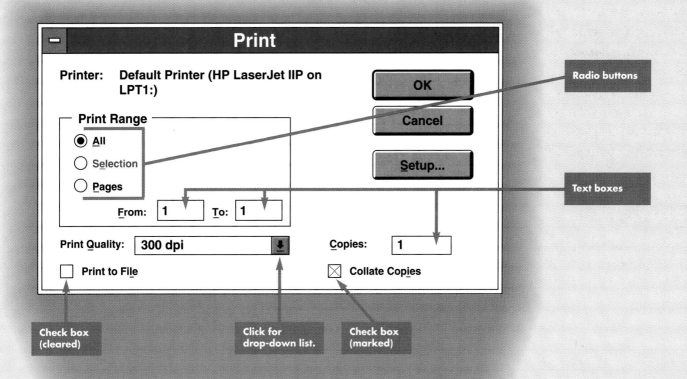

Radio buttons

Text boxes

Check box (cleared)

Click for drop-down list.

Check box (marked)

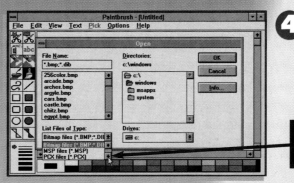

4 A downward-pointing arrow with a horizontal line below it means you can click on the arrow to see a *drop-down list* of options. When you spot the option you need, click on it.

Click here to scroll through the drop-down list.

CHAPTER 3

Welcome to Microsoft Works

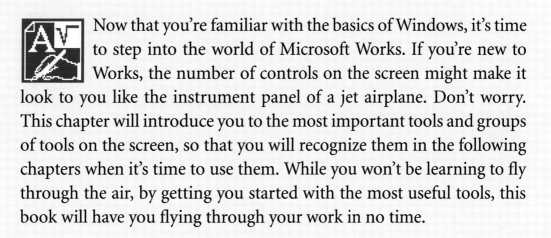 Now that you're familiar with the basics of Windows, it's time to step into the world of Microsoft Works. If you're new to Works, the number of controls on the screen might make it look to you like the instrument panel of a jet airplane. Don't worry. This chapter will introduce you to the most important tools and groups of tools on the screen, so that you will recognize them in the following chapters when it's time to use them. While you won't be learning to fly through the air, by getting you started with the most useful tools, this book will have you flying through your work in no time.

How to Get Started in Microsoft Works

Whenever you start Microsoft Works, one of the first things you'll see is the Startup dialog box. After you select the part of Works you want to work with, you'll see a screen much like the one in the large illustration to the right. It shows the word processor with a new document window. If you're working with only one document, as you will be throughout most of this book, you'll have a little more elbow room if you maximize both the document and application windows. If you see a Restore button in the upper-right corner of either window, then it is already maximized. (See Chapter 2 if you need help maximizing your windows.) Most of the illustrations in this book, including the ones in this chapter, have maximized application and document windows.

TIP SHEET

▶ The *status bar* gives you helpful clues about what you can do in your document. As you try typing, highlighting menu items, or moving the mouse over buttons in the toolbar, the status bar will display different messages.

▶ If you need more space in the work area, you can hide the toolbar by opening the View menu and then clicking on Toolbar to remove the check mark next to it. Beginners and experts agree, however, that using the toolbar is often the most efficient way to work. If the toolbar doesn't appear on your screen and you want it to, you can show it the same way you hide it: Click on the View menu, and then on Toolbar, this time to check the menu item.

▶ Help is always available in Microsoft Works when you need it. If necessary, you can make selections from the Help menu just like any other menu, but you'll see more on help in the next chapter

1 To start Microsoft Works, first start Windows. Next open the program group containing Microsoft Works and double-click on the Microsoft Works icon. (See Chapter 2 if you need help with these operations.)

8 The work area in the document window is where you will perform most of your computing activities. Typing documents, performing calculations, and communicating with remote computers are just some of the things you will do here.

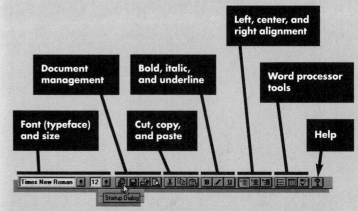

7 You can perform common actions quickly and easily by clicking the buttons on the toolbar. The icon on each button gives a graphical representation of what the button does. If you move your mouse pointer over any of the buttons without clicking, a small box will appear below the pointer to show you the button's name.

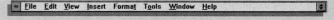

6 The menu bar in Works shows these eight menu names except when you're in the communications package. Click on a menu name to pull down the menu. You can then either select an item in the menu by clicking on it or close the menu without making a selection by clicking outside it.

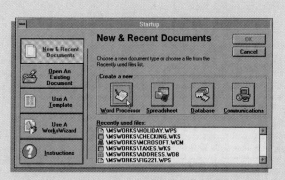

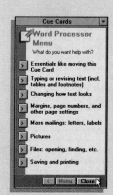

2 The first time you start Works after installation, you'll see the Welcome to Microsoft Works dialog box. Click one of the large rectangular buttons to take a guided tour of Works, start Works without the tour for the time being, or skip the welcome screen every time you start up in the future.

3 If you have chosen to skip the tour, you'll see the Startup dialog box. Click one of the large square buttons in the "Create a new" area to start one of the four main parts of Works.

4 Hide the Cue Cards window for the time being. To do this, click on the Close button in the lower-right corner of the Cue Cards window.

Control Menu box (application window)

Combined title bar (for application and document windows)

Minimize button (application window)

Control Menu box (document window)

Restore button (application window)

Ruler (word processor only)

Restore button (document window)

Mouse pointer (I-beam)

Toolbar (showing word processor tools)

Work area

Vertical scroll bar

Status bar

Horizontal scroll bar

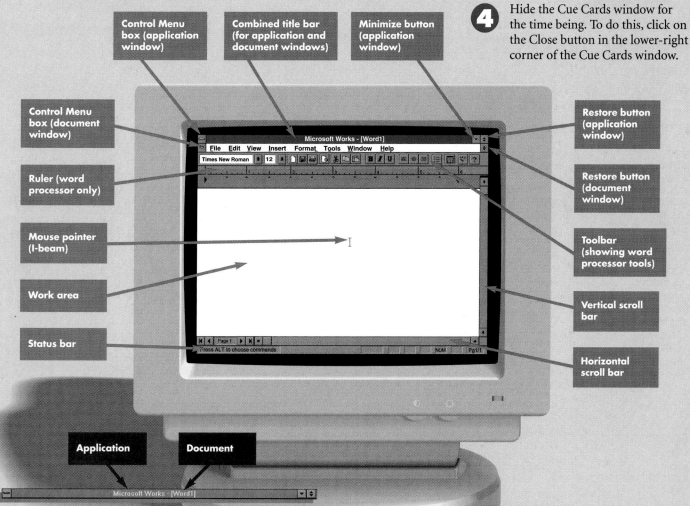

Application

Document

5 When the document window is maximized, the title bar shows both the name of the application running in the window, "Microsoft Works," and the name of the maximized document active in that program. When you create a new word processor document, Works will call it "Word1" until you save and name it. (A new spreadsheet document is called "Sheet1," a new database document is called "Data1," and a new communications document is called "Comm1.")

CHAPTER 4

Creating a Document with the Word Processor

 By now you should already be familiar with Microsoft Windows and have a pretty good idea of what you can do with Microsoft Works. Of all the things Works can do, word processing is probably the most important. You can use the word processor for almost everything: from jotting down your ideas, to organizing them, to formatting them and showing them off. You can use the spreadsheet, the database, and other tools for their specialized purposes, but when it comes time to put all the pieces together, the word processor is the place you'll do it.

In this chapter, you'll learn the basics of word processing. Creating new documents, saving them, retrieving saved documents, and printing are covered here, too, since these skills are necessary and useful throughout Windows. Finally, you'll see the proper way to shut down Works and your computer when you're finished. When you finish this introduction to the word processor, you'll know enough to complete much of your computer work, so turn the page!

How to Create a New Word Processor Document

When you write a letter or other document, you'll have to begin somewhere. You've already taken the hardest step by sitting down in front of your computer, so the next step of creating a new document window in Works should be a little easier. The new document window looks blank, but there's really quite a bit there that you can't see immediately. Works starts your document with default settings for everything from the font, or typeface, to the tab stops. You'll learn to change these settings in later chapters, but for now it will be easier to take advantage of what Works has already set up for you.

TIP SHEET

▶ **Microsoft apparently believes that you can have too much of a good thing, since they limit the number of documents you can open at one time to eight. This is plenty for doing just about anything you can imagine. Besides, too many open windows can be confusing and may slow down your computer.**

▶ **If you don't see the toolbar on your screen, you can still create a new document with the Startup dialog box. Simply click on the File menu name to pull down the menu, and click again on Create New File to display the Startup dialog box.**

1 Start Works if you haven't already done so by double-clicking on the Microsoft Works icon in Program Manager. If you see the Welcome to Microsoft Works dialog box, click on the Start Works Now button.

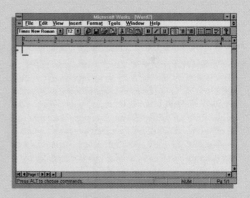

5 Once you've started and maximized your second document window, your screen should look like this. Notice that the document is named Word2, since it was the second new word-processor document created in this session of Microsoft Works.

2 In the Startup dialog box you'll see that the New & Recent Documents button in the upper-left corner of the dialog box is depressed. When this button is depressed (the default), you'll also see a group of four square buttons across the right-center of the dialog box. This group is named "Create a new." Click the square Word Processor button to create a new word processor document.

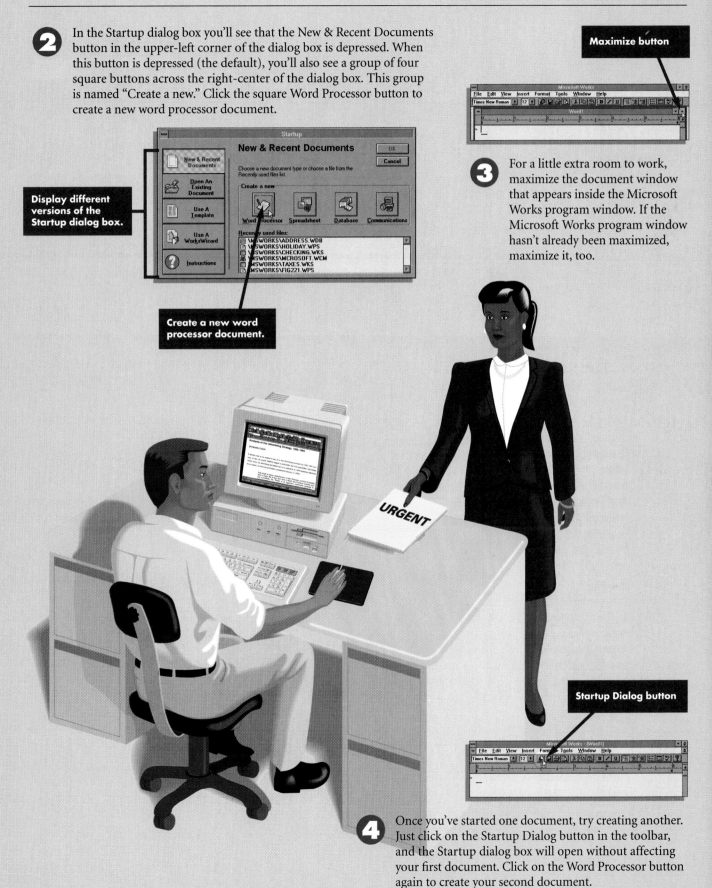

Maximize button

Display different versions of the Startup dialog box.

Create a new word processor document.

3 For a little extra room to work, maximize the document window that appears inside the Microsoft Works program window. If the Microsoft Works program window hasn't already been maximized, maximize it, too.

Startup Dialog button

4 Once you've started one document, try creating another. Just click on the Startup Dialog button in the toolbar, and the Startup dialog box will open without affecting your first document. Click on the Word Processor button again to create your second document.

How to Type in Text

Typing with the word processor of Microsoft Works is very similar to working with a typewriter. But in addition, the word processor handles many little typing tasks for you, such as figuring out if another word will fit at the end of a line. There are slight differences between typing on a typewriter and a word processor. Once you know them, though, you'll be on your way to proficient word processing.

TIP SHEET

▶ If you've just made a typo, you can erase it quickly and easily. Just back up with the Backspace key and type the correct letter or word.

▶ If you're accustomed to using a typewriter, you'll soon discover that the Caps Lock button on your computer keyboard doesn't work like you might expect. On a typewriter, you lock capital letters with the Caps Lock key and unlock them with the Shift key. On most word processors, including the one in Microsoft Works, you lock capital letters in the usual way, but you unlock them by pressing the Caps Lock key a second time.

▶ When you set a tab stop on the ruler, you'll notice two things. First, the tab stop you set doesn't look like any of the others. That's because there are two kinds of tab stops in Works: *default* and *user-defined*. Default tab stops look like a little upside-down T. User-defined tab stops look like an L with an arrow on top. Both behave in pretty much the same way as tab stops on a typewriter. The second thing you'll notice is that there are no default tab stops to the left of your user-defined stops. That's because Works assumes that the tabs you set are the first ones you want to stop at. This is very handy when you want to set a single tab halfway or farther across the page.

▶ Custom tab settings are a type of *paragraph formatting*, which works on only one paragraph at a time. As a result, you might notice that the tabs you set in one paragraph disappear when you click in another paragraph.

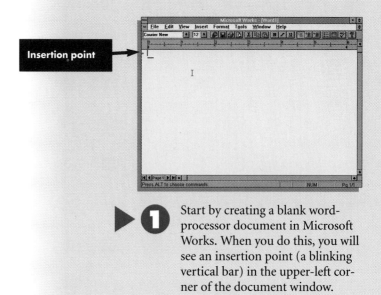

Insertion point

1 Start by creating a blank word-processor document in Microsoft Works. When you do this, you will see an insertion point (a blinking vertical bar) in the upper-left corner of the document window.

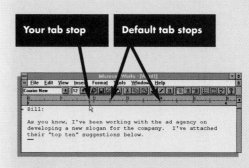

Your tab stop   Default tab stops

5 Tab stops are adjusted on a typewriter with the Tab Set and Tab Clear keys. In Works, you set a tab stop by clicking the mouse on the bottom half of the ruler. To move a tab stop, click on it and drag it to the desired position. To clear a tab stop, click on it and drag it off of the ruler.

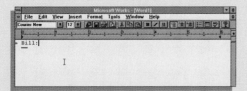

2 The insertion point shows you where the next letter you type will appear in the document window. If you don't already, think of the work area of the document window as a sheet of paper. The letters you type on the keyboard will appear in the work area just like letters you type on a typewriter appear on your paper.

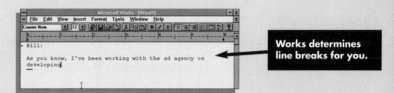

Works determines line breaks for you.

3 Try typing a few lines of text. You can type anything you want, but if your imagination isn't in high gear right now, you are welcome to copy the text in the central graphic. Notice how Works determines what words will fit on a line and which word should start the next line. With Works, you'll never have to strain to hear the end-of-line bell, only to discover when it rings that you can't finish the word you've just started.

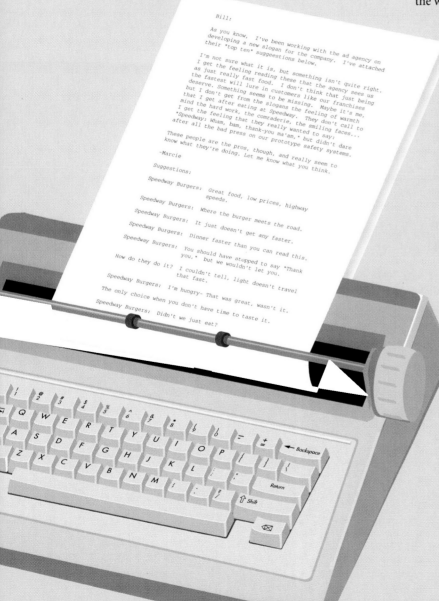

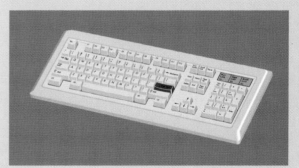

4 Your computer keyboard doesn't have a carriage-return key like a typewriter's. Instead, it has an Enter key, which works somewhat differently. You won't need it to end every line at the right margin, but when you want to end a line early and start a new one, as at the end of a paragraph, the Enter key is just what you need.

How to Save and Retrieve a Document

As mentioned in Chapter 2, your computer has two types of memory. It has short-term memory, called random-access memory (RAM), and it has long-term storage, generally a hard disk. When you create a document in Microsoft Works, you are creating it in RAM. You do this because RAM remembers and recalls information very quickly. The trouble is, when you turn off your computer, RAM forgets everything you told it. Everything.

For Works to remember your document when you turn off your computer, you first need to save it to your hard disk. Saving documents to disk allows your computer to remember them days, weeks, or even years later, so that they can be retrieved to the faster RAM when you need them again.

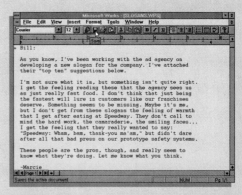

▶ **1** The easiest way to save a document is to use the Save button on the toolbar, so move the mouse pointer over it and click the left mouse button once.

TIP SHEET

▶ **After you have saved a document for the first time, you won't be asked to name it when you use the Save button again.**

▶ **If you want to rename a document after saving it, select the Save As command in the File menu. Works will open the Save As dialog box again for you so you can type in a new name.**

▶ **There's an alternative for reopening documents, too. Click on the File menu to open it and then select Open Existing File. You'll see the Open dialog box, which is much like the Save As dialog box. Once it is open, double-click on the name of the file you want to open in the File Name list box on the left side.**

▶ **If you're in the Startup dialog box and don't see the file you want to open, click on the large Open An Existing Document button on the left side to see the Open dialog box.**

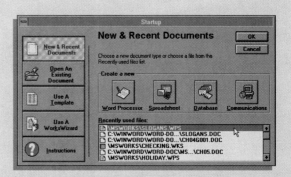

6 In the lower-right corner of the dialog box is the "Recently used files" list box. The file name you just saved should be at the top of the list. Double-click on the file to reopen it.

2 If this is the first time you're saving this document, the Save As dialog box will open next. Click once in the File Name box in the upper-left corner of the dialog box, and type in a name of up to eight letters (be sure not to include any spaces or punctuation). Works will add a period and a three-character extension (.WPS) to the file name for you.

3 Click on the OK button. Your document will be saved to your hard disk where you can retrieve it whenever you want.

4 Close your document by clicking twice on the document Control Menu box.

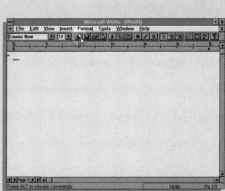

5 If you don't have any other documents open, you'll see the Startup dialog box. If you do have another open, click once on the Startup Dialog button in the toolbar.

How to Print a Document

It would be nice if you could type in your document, save it to your hard disk, and then electronically mail it to everyone who needed to see it. It would be nice, too, if the text on a monitor were as clean and crisp as text on paper, and were as enjoyable to read and manipulate as a good book. This all may be possible someday, but unfortunately, not yet.

Since the paperless office is still a long way off, you'll want to occasionally show your boss why she's paying you and print the document on your screen.

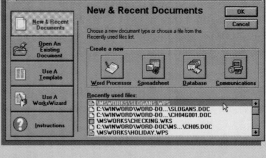

1 To print the document, you'll first need to have it on your screen. Start by retrieving an old document or creating a new one.

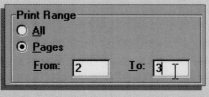

7 Click in the To box just to the right and type in the number of the last page you want to print. Send the pages to the printer by clicking the OK button.

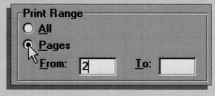

6 In the Print Range box, click on the Pages option button. The cursor will move to the From box, where you type in the first page you want to print out.

2 Review the document first, so that you won't waste paper by having to print it again, and second, to be sure you won't be embarrassed if the wrong person gets to the printer before you do. When you're ready, click on the Print button.

3 If you want to do something special, like print multiple copies of your document or only a few of its pages, select the File menu, and then click on the Print option. The Print dialog box will open.

4 To print multiple copies, just type in the number you want. Works expects you to print one copy, but when the dialog box opens, the Number of Copies box is active, waiting for you to tell it something different. When you're finished, click the OK button to print your document.

5 To print just a few of the pages in your document (a handy feature if you've just corrected a mistake), you must first decide what range of pages you need to print. With that in mind, open the Print dialog box as you did in step 3.

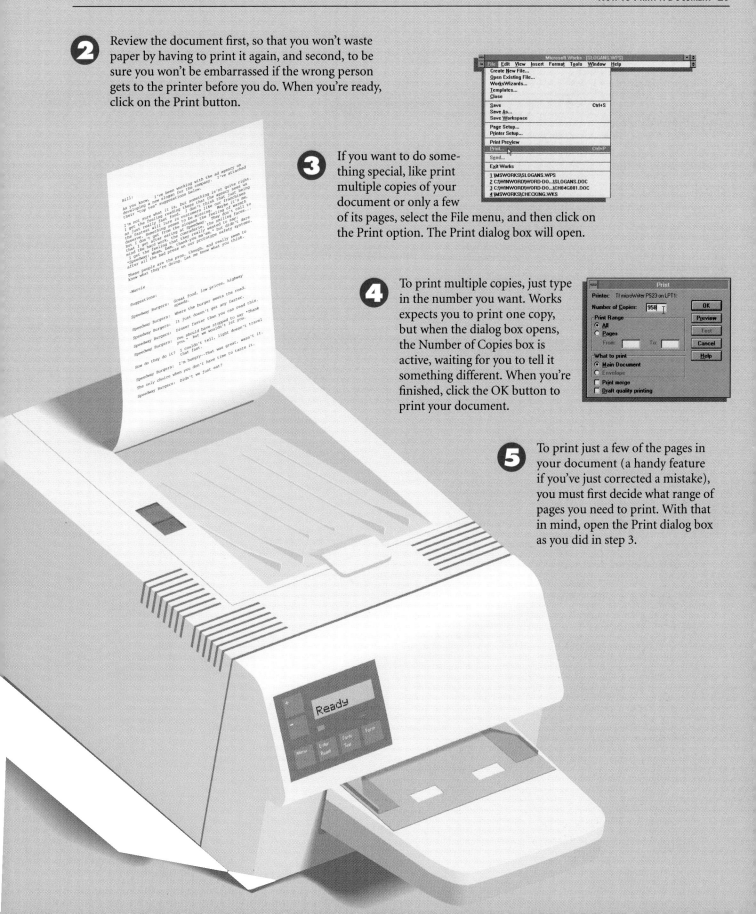

How to Exit Microsoft Works

It's the end of the day, you've been working hard and been extremely productive with your newly learned word processing skills. It's time to shut down the computer and go home, but panic seizes you as you realize that you don't know how to exit Works! This is a joke, of course. You could just turn your computer off and walk away, but there's a better, safer solution. Just turning off the computer would be like getting ready for bed by just turning out the light. You'll sleep better if you do a few things first.

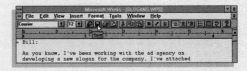

▶ **1** The first step is to save your work. Clicking the Save button on the toolbar is the easiest way to do that.

▶ The end of the day is a good time to create a backup (or second copy) of the document you're working on. Select the Save As command in the File menu and give your document a name you'll understand, like "May12." That way, if you accidentally save changes that you don't want to keep, you'll have an earlier version to fall back on.

▶ If you want to have all of the documents you're working on opened for you automatically the next time you start Works, save and leave open those documents and select Save Workspace from the File menu. Works will remember all the documents open at that time and ready them for you the next time you start it up.

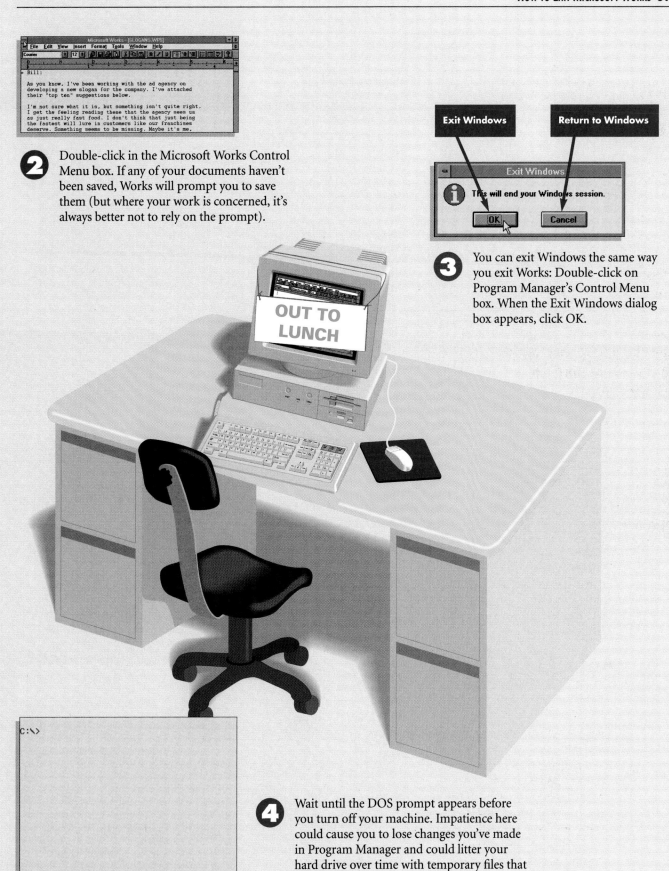

Exit Windows

Return to Windows

Exit Windows

This will end your Windows session.

OK   Cancel

2 Double-click in the Microsoft Works Control Menu box. If any of your documents haven't been saved, Works will prompt you to save them (but where your work is concerned, it's always better not to rely on the prompt).

3 You can exit Windows the same way you exit Works: Double-click on Program Manager's Control Menu box. When the Exit Windows dialog box appears, click OK.

4 Wait until the DOS prompt appears before you turn off your machine. Impatience here could cause you to lose changes you've made in Program Manager and could litter your hard drive over time with temporary files that were never deleted.

How to Get Help

Perhaps the most comforting feature of Works is its extensive help library. It contains answers to almost every question you can think up. While many of the help features aim at getting beginning users up and running, you'll never outgrow the help library. For many people, just the opposite is true: The more experience they have with Works, the more things they want to tweak to get a desired effect.

TIP SHEET

▶ In Chapter 3 you turned off Cue Cards. If you would like to use Works with a cheat sheet by your side, then give them a try. Simply select Cue Cards from the Help menu.

▶ If you like Cue Cards, but find that they block the view of your document, then click on the Minimize button in the Cue Cards window. Works will minimize the window and leave an icon on top of your document. Double-click the icon to restore the Cue Cards window when you need more help.

▶ In addition to a table of contents, Help also has an index. If you know the name of the topic you want help on, select "Search for Help on" in the Help menu. Type in the term at the top of the Search dialog box, and double-click to select from the broad topics that appear in the top list box. Finally, double-click again to select a specific topic in the bottom list box. A Help window will open, allowing you to read about the topic of your choice.

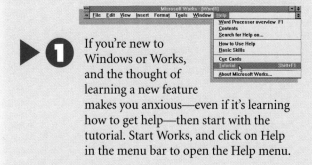

1 If you're new to Windows or Works, and the thought of learning a new feature makes you anxious—even if it's learning how to get help—then start with the tutorial. Start Works, and click on Help in the menu bar to open the Help menu.

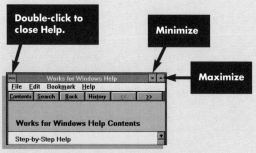

8 You can treat the Help window like any other application window. You can minimize it or maximize it with the appropriate window button, or you can close it by double-clicking on the Control Menu box.

7 Words underlined with a dotted line will display a pop-up definition or a brief explanation when you click on them.

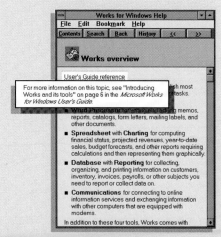

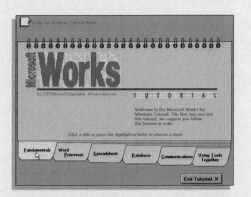

3 The first time through, follow the tutorials in order. Click on the leftmost tab, Fundamentals, and select from the options that Works gives you. To choose a lesson, click on one of the small square buttons next to a text option. You can proceed through each lesson at your own pace.

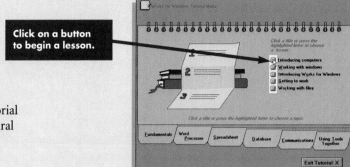

Click on a button to begin a lesson.

2 In the Help menu, click on Tutorial. The Tutorial window will open, showing the image of a spiral notebook with tabs at the bottom.

4 To move through the lessons, select from the buttons at the bottom of each page to move forward or backward, or to select from a list of other options.

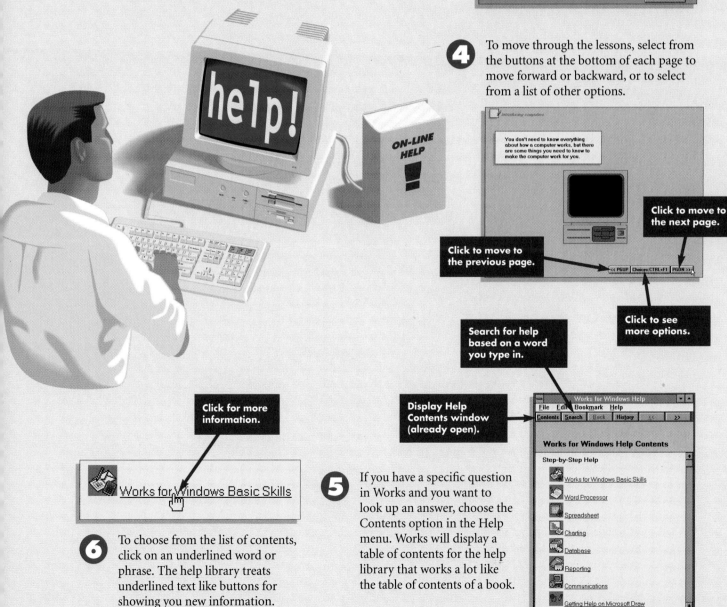

Click to move to the next page.

Click to move to the previous page.

Click to see more options.

Search for help based on a word you type in.

Display Help Contents window (already open).

Click for more information.

Works for Windows Basic Skills

5 If you have a specific question in Works and you want to look up an answer, choose the Contents option in the Help menu. Works will display a table of contents for the help library that works a lot like the table of contents of a book.

6 To choose from the list of contents, click on an underlined word or phrase. The help library treats underlined text like buttons for showing you new information.

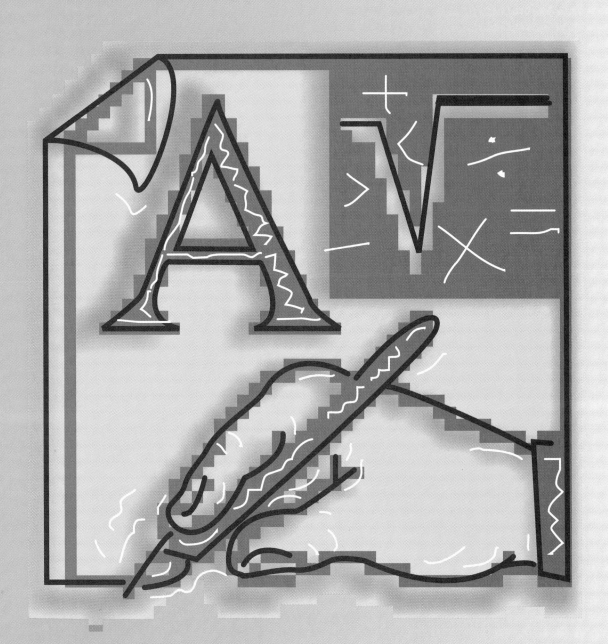

CHAPTER 5

Editing Text in a Document

In its most basic form, editing is simply correcting mistakes in your document. Perhaps you have misspelled a word and need to correct it, or maybe you have typed a word twice or left one out. Either way, you probably need to go back and retype a little.

In a slightly elevated form, editing can mean reorganizing and re-arranging the text you have typed. Perhaps you need to explain one idea before introducing another. Maybe you omitted a concept or wrote it in a redundant fashion. In these cases, you may need to make substantial revisions, often by moving blocks of text from one location to another in your document.

Editing can get far more complex, but at these levels, the changes you need to make don't have to be difficult or time-consuming. If you were working with a typewriter, you might have to start from scratch and retype your entire document. With a word processor, however, changes that might otherwise take hours can be done with just a few simple mouse movements. With Microsoft Works, the only difficult part of editing is deciding what changes to make.

How to Select Text

To select text is to mark one or more charac-ters for action. What kind of action? After selecting text you can delete it, move it, format it—the list goes on. This page explains how to select text. Starting on the next page and con-tinuing throughout this book, you will learn about the many actions you can perform on text and other objects after selecting them.

TIP SHEET

▶ **To select text using the keyboard, first use the arrow keys to position the inser-tion point at one end of the text block. Then, hold down the Shift key and use the arrow keys to move toward the other end of the block, highlighting text as you go. Release the Shift key when the complete block is selected.**

▶ **To select a complete line or paragraph, position the mouse pointer in the left margin next to the line or paragraph you want to select. The mouse pointer becomes an arrow. Then click once to select the line, or double-click to select the paragraph. To select a word, double-click on it.**

▶ **To deselect text without performing an action on it, click anywhere in the work area of the window. Or, with the key-board, release the Shift key and then press any arrow key.**

▶ **When you drag to select text, Works automatically selects whole words. If you want to select only parts of words, click on the Tools menu, select the Options command, and then click in the Automatic Word Selection check box to remove the check mark and turn off the feature. Click OK to close the dialog box.**

▶ **1** Locate the text you want to select. If possible, scroll the document so that the entire block to be selected is in view. If you need a quick reminder on scrolling, see "How to Use the Mouse in Windows" in Chapter 2.

Select a sentence (or any amount of text) to apply a command to that block only.

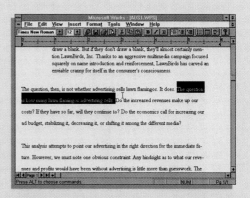

 5 Release the mouse button. The text remains selected. Now you can issue commands that affect only this text.

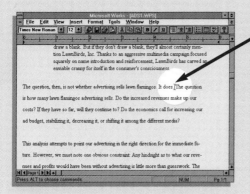

Start of block

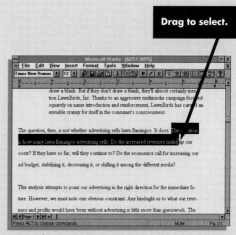

Drag to select.

2 Position the mouse pointer at one end of the block.

3 Holding down the left mouse button, drag the mouse toward the other end of the block. As you drag over text, it becomes highlighted, indicating that it is selected.

LawnBirds, Inc.

ANALYSIS OF OUR ADVERTISING STRATEGY, 1992–1994

INTRODUCTION

It should come as no surprise to any of us that advertising increased our 1992–1994 revenues. In fact, the graphs attached suggest a predictable and even quantifiable relationship. What's more, our advertising has helped earn us a reputation in a field populated otherwise by no-names. As *Advertising Punditry* commented (January 12, 1994):

> Ask people to name a manufacturer of lawn flamingos and they'll probably draw a blank. But if they don't draw a blank, they'll almost certainly mention LawnBirds, Inc. Thanks to an aggressive multimedia campaign focused squarely on name introduction and reinforcement, LawnBirds has carved an enviable cranny for itself in the consumer's consciousness.

The question, then, is not *whether* advertising sells lawn flamingos. It does. The question is *how many* lawn flamingos advertising sells. Do the increased revenues make up our costs? If they have so far, will they continue to? Do the economics call for increasing our ad budget, stabilizing it, decreasing it, or shifting it among the different media?

This analysis attempts to point our advertising in the right direction for the immediate future. However, we must note one obvious constraint: Any hindsight as to what our revenues and profits would have been without advertising is little more than guesswork. The most we can do is project our growth from our preadvertising years and factor in those marketplace changes that we understand and that are quantifiable.

Why did we start advertising in the first place? It's worthwhile occasionally to remind ourselves why we took the path we took. Recall that in 1991 we saw the arrival of several competitors, many of them with low operating costs and excellent contacts within our

Drag back to reduce the selection.

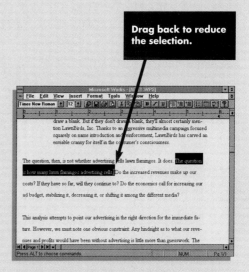

4 If you select too much text, drag the other way to unselect it.

How to Delete Text

To make changes to text in Microsoft Works, you'll often have to delete the old text first. You can delete one character at a time or make a mass deletion by selecting text first. Text to the right of the deletion point shifts left to fill the vacated space, and line breaks adjust automatically.

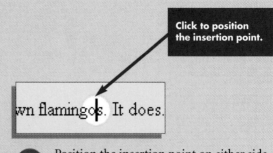

Click to position the insertion point.

▶ **1** Position the insertion point on either side of the first character you want to delete. Or, select a block of text (see preceding page) if you want to delete the whole block.

TIP SHEET

▶ Most system setups allow you to delete the selected block and immediately start replacing it with other text by simply typing. If this feature does not work on your computer and you want to use it, click on Tools in the menu bar and then click on Options. Near the top center of the Options dialog box, click on the Typing Replaces Selection check box. Then click on the OK button to return to your document.

▶ If you simply want to replace text, you can type over it. Move the cursor to the beginning of the text you want to replace, and press the Insert key (labeled *Ins* on some keyboards). You'll see the letters *OVR* appear near the right end of the status bar, meaning Works is in overtype mode. Each character you now type will replace the next character to the right of the insertion point. When you are through, be sure to press the Insert key again to return to insert mode.

Delete key

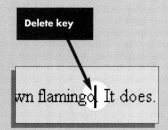

2 To delete the character to the right of the insertion point, press the Delete key (labeled *Del* on some keyboards).

Backspace key

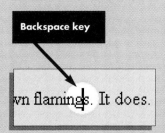

3 To delete the character to the left of the insertion point, press the Backspace key.

LawnBirds, Inc.

ANALYSIS OF OUR ADVERTISING STRATEGY, 1992–1994

INTRODUCTION

It should come as no surprise to any of us that advertising increased our 1992–1994 revenues. In fact, the graphs attached suggest a predictable and even quantifiable relationship. What's more, our advertising has helped earn us a reputation in a field populated otherwise by no-names. As *Advertising Punditry* commented (January 12, 1994):

> Ask people to name a manufacturer of lawn flamingos and they'll probably draw a blank. But if they don't draw a blank, they'll almost certainly mention LawnBirds, Inc. Thanks to an aggressive multimedia campaign focused squarely on name introduction and reinforcement, LawnBirds has carved an enviable cranny for itself in the consumer's consciousness.

The question, then, is not *whether* advertising sells lawn flamingos. It does. ~~The question is *how many* lawn flamingos advertising sells.~~ Do the increased revenues make up our costs? If they have so far, will they continue to? Do the economics call for increasing our ad budget, stabilizing it, decreasing it, or shifting it among the different media?

This analysis attempts to point our advertising in the right direction for the immediate future. However, we must note one obvious constraint: Any hindsight as to what our revenues and profits would have been without advertising is little more than guesswork. The most we can do is project our growth from our preadvertising years and factor in those marketplace changes that we understand and that are quantifiable.

Why did we start advertising in the first place? It's worthwhile occasionally to remind ourselves why we took the path we took. Recall that in 1991 we saw the arrival of several competitors, many of them with low operating costs and excellent contacts within our

Backspace or Delete

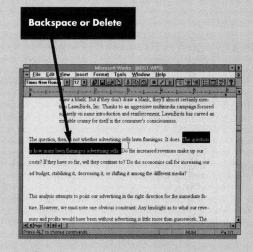

4 To delete the selected block, press the Backspace key or the Delete key.

5 If you delete text accidentally, immediately press Ctrl+Z to activate the Undo feature. Some or all of the deleted text may return so you don't have to retype it.

How to Navigate through a Document

Most documents are too long to display on your screen all at once. To work with large documents, Works gives you two basic methods to move, or navigate, through them. The first way to navigate is to move the insertion point (see steps 1 through 5). The insertion point, of course, is where you add and delete text.

The second way to navigate is to show different parts of the document in the document window (see steps 6 through 8). Try thinking of the Works document window as just that: a window that lets you see a part of your document. You can't move the window around in front of the document, but you can move the document around behind the window to let different parts show through.

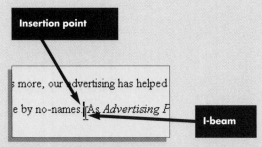

1 The easiest way to move the insertion point in a window is to point with the I-beam mouse pointer where you want to put the insertion point, and then click.

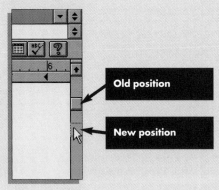

7 Click and drag the scroll box to move the document view anywhere in the document. The length of the vertical scroll bar represents the length of your document, so if you drag two-thirds of the way down the scroll bar and let go of the mouse button, Works will move you two-thirds of the way through your document.

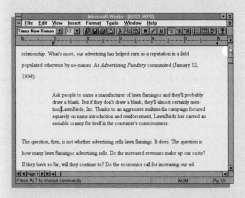

6 Click on the vertical scroll bar between the scroll box and either of its ends to move the view up and down by the amount you can see in the document window. (Use the horizontal scroll bar to move left and right one window width at a time.)

TIP SHEET

▶ Hold down the Shift key while you use any of the navigation keys on the keyboard, and you'll select text as you move. For example, the Shift+End key combination selects all of the text from the insertion point to the end of its line.

▶ The fastest way to select very large blocks of text is to drag the scroll box: Click at the beginning of the block you want to highlight, drag the scroll box to the end of the block, and then hold down the Shift key while you click again with the mouse at the end of the block. Works will highlight all of the text between your two clicks.

2 The arrow keys on the keyboard let you move the insertion point one step in any direction. The up and down arrows move one line at a time, while the left and right arrows move one space at a time.

3 The Home and End keys move the insertion point to the beginning and end of the current line. The PgUp and PgDn keys move *both* the insertion point and the window view up and down by the amount you can see in the document window. If you change the size of the document window, you'll change the distance that these keys move you as well.

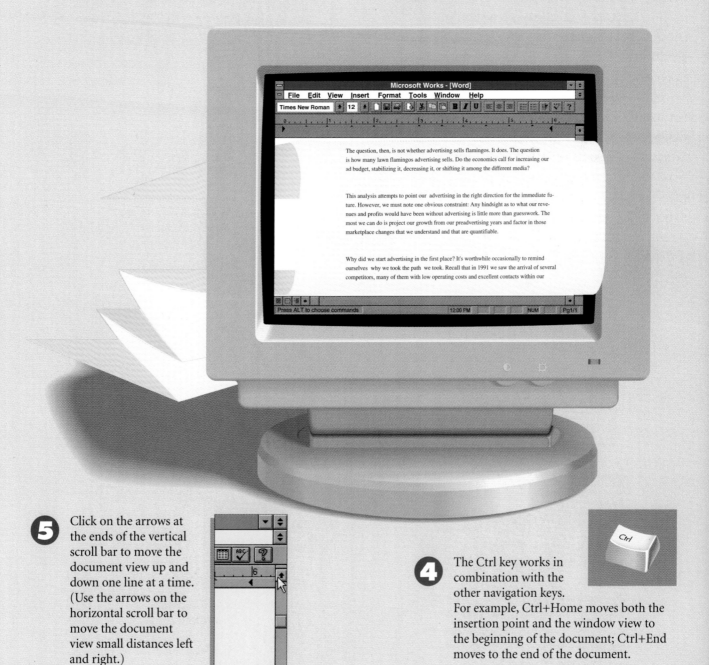

5 Click on the arrows at the ends of the vertical scroll bar to move the document view up and down one line at a time. (Use the arrows on the horizontal scroll bar to move the document view small distances left and right.)

4 The Ctrl key works in combination with the other navigation keys. For example, Ctrl+Home moves both the insertion point and the window view to the beginning of the document; Ctrl+End moves to the end of the document.

How to Move Text

You'll sometimes find that you've typed in exactly what you intended to say, but in the wrong order. The next time this happens to you, don't bother retyping everything. Works gives you two ways to move blocks of text from one location in your document to another: *drag and drop* and *cut and paste*. Drag and drop is the easiest way to move blocks of text short distances in your document. Cut and paste, on the other hand, takes advantage of the Windows Clipboard, making it easier to move text long distances in your document, or even between the four main parts of Works (see Chapter 14).

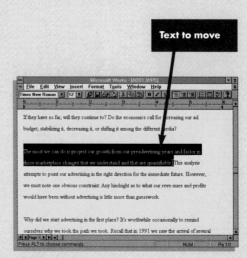

Text to move

1 To move a block of text using drag and drop, you first need to tell Works which block you want to move. Click and drag to highlight it.

6 Move the insertion point to the text destination by clicking once. Now from the Edit menu, select Paste. Works will insert the cut text from the Clipboard into the new location.

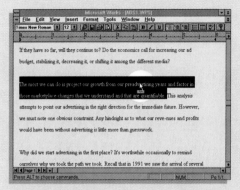

2 To move the text, click once on the highlighted text and hold down the mouse button. The standard I-beam pointer will change to the *DRAG pointer.*

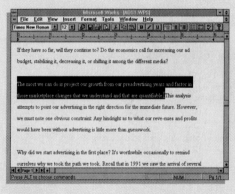

Destination

3 Without letting go of the button, drag the mouse pointer and the attached insertion point to the new location for the text. The DRAG pointer will change to the *MOVE pointer.* When you reach the right spot, release the mouse button, and Works will move the text for you.

ANALYSIS OF OUR ADVERTISING STRATEGY, 1992-1994

INTRODUCTION

It should come as no surprise to any of us that advertising increased our 1992-1994 revenues. In fact, the graphs attached suggest a predictable and even quantifiable relationship. What's more, our advertising has helped earn us a reputation in a field populated otherwise by no-names. As *Advertising Pundrity* commented (January 12, 1994):

Ask people to name a manufacturer of lawn flamingos and they'll probably draw a blank. But if they don't draw a blank, they'll almost certainly mention LawnBirds, Inc. Thanks to an aggressive multimedia campaign focused squarely on name introduction and reinforcement, LawnBirds has carved an enviable cranny for itself in the consumer's consciousness.

The question, then, is not whether advertising sells lawn flamingos. It does. The question is how many lawn flamingos advertising sells. Do the increased revenues [...] our costs? If they have so far, will they continue to? Do the economics call for [...] ing ad budget, stabilizing it, decreasing it, or shifting it among the different me[...]

The question, then, is not wheather advertising can sell lawn flamingoes. It does. [...]diate future. However, we must note one obvious constraint: Any hindsight as to what [...] nues and profits would have been without advertising is little more than guesswork. The most we can do is project our growth from our preadvertising years and factor in those marketplace changes that we understand and that are quantifiable.

Why did we start advertising in the first place? It's worthwhile occasionally to remind ourselves why we took the path we took. Recall that in 1991 we saw the arrival of several competitors, many of them with low operating costs and excellent contacts within our

4 To move a block of text using cut and paste, first select the block of text to move.

5 Click on the Edit menu, and then the Cut command. Works will move the text to the Windows Clipboard. The Windows Clipboard acts as a temporary holding spot for just about any kind of data. In this case, it's text.

CHAPTER 6

Text Enhancement

Give your characters some character and watch your documents shine. Boldface, italics, font changes, and other text enhancements can make important text stand out and give your documents a more professional look.

Not that character formatting has aesthetic value only. Sometimes convention demands it. For example, by convention, references to foreign-language words are printed in italics.

This chapter and the next cover Works's major character, paragraph, and page formatting features, so some advice is in order: Don't over-format your documents. A page crowded with text styles, margin changes, different type sizes, and other attention-getters is likely to backfire by becoming unattractive and difficult to read. Tinkering excessively with the formatting of an unimportant document is a real time-waster, too. Apply formatting judiciously when and where it will have an impact.

How to Boldface, Italicize, and Underline Text

Boldface is probably the best way to emphasize a short block of text. Most headlines you see in publications are in boldface.

Italic type usually indicates new vocabulary, foreign-language words, and publication titles.

Underline substitutes for italics in handwriting and in type where italic type is unavailable.

Since the procedures for applying boldface, italic, and underline are nearly identical, you'll see the details on applying only boldface here.

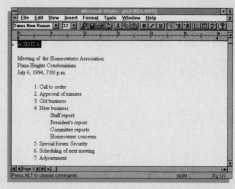

1 Type the text you want to boldface, and then select it. It can be any amount of text, from one character to an entire document.

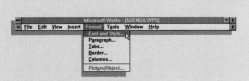

2 Click on Format in the menu bar and then click on the Font and Style command.

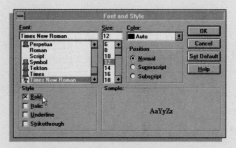

3 In the Style area, in the lower-left corner of the dialog box, click on the Bold check box to select it.

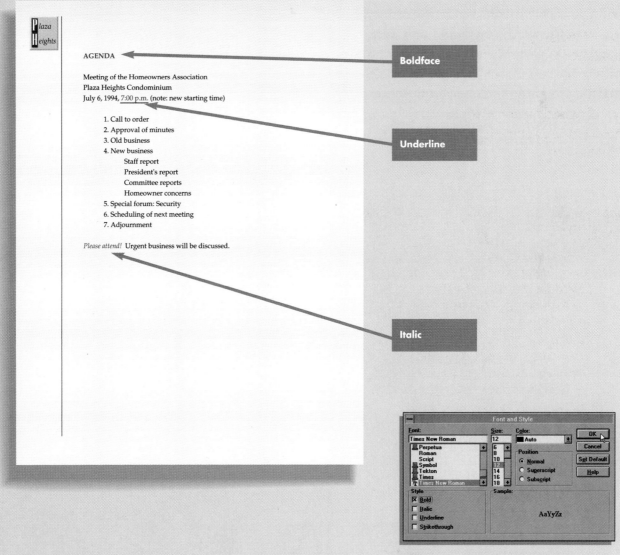

Boldface

Underline

Italic

4 Click on the OK button.

How to Change Fonts

What fonts you have available depends on such factors as your printer and your version of Windows. No matter—Works knows exactly what fonts you have and makes it easy for you to choose among them. Prudent use of fonts can make for truly handsome documents. Most type experts advise sticking to two fonts per document, perhaps one font for heading and one for body text. Then apply other text styles such as boldface and size changes to make other distinctions. For example, you might pick one font for all the headings in your document, and use different type sizes to show different heading levels.

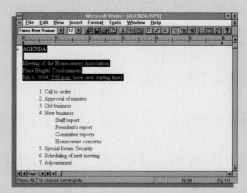

▶ **1** Type and select the text whose font you want to change. It can be any amount of text, from one character to an entire document.

TIP SHEET

▶ Technically, a font is a set of characters in one typeface, size, and style (such as bold, italic, or regular). However, most people use font as a synonym for typeface; this book follows the same convention.

▶ Works offers a command to instantly select the whole document for an operation such as a font change. Click on Edit in the menu bar and click on the Select All command. Then change the font as described on this page.

▶ The entries in the Font and Style dialog box normally show you the formatting in effect for the currently selected text, but sometimes an entry is blank or gray. Observe, for example, the Style entries in step 3 on this page. The shaded check boxes mean that there is more than one relevant formatting option in effect for the currently selected text. In the example, the currently selected text includes the bold-faced word "Agenda," the underlined "7:00 p.m.," and several lines of regular text. You specify a formatting option for the selected text the same way (as described in this chapter) whether or not the entry is blank or gray.

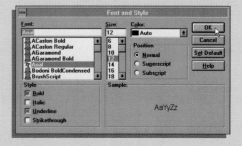

5 Click on the OK button.

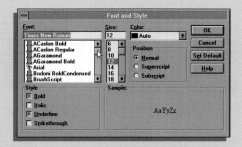

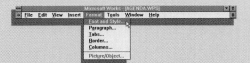

2 Click on Format in the menu bar and then click on the Font and Style command.

3 The Font list in the upper-left corner of the dialog box shows you all of your available fonts. Locate the font you need. You may have to scroll the list.

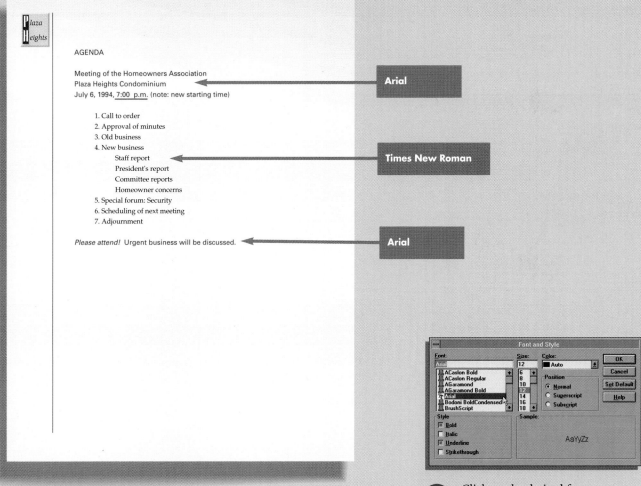

4 Click on the desired font.

How to Change Text Size

Most type you read in books and periodicals is 10, 11, or 12 points high. (There are 72 points to an inch.) Large type—especially when combined with boldface—is ideal for headlines and announcements. Small type is available for the proverbial "fine print."

TIP SHEET

▶ **Normally, the Font and Style dialog box displays only those point sizes that your printer can print in the font of the currently selected text. If the selected text contains more than one font, however, the Font dialog box may let you select point sizes that your printer cannot print in every font you are using. Therefore, in a document containing a variety of fonts and point sizes, you should check your printouts to make sure the point sizes came out as you planned. If some text was not printed in the desired size, you may have to change its font to one that has a greater variety of point sizes available on your printer.**

▶ **Beware that small variations in type size often go unnoticed by the reader, while extreme variations may be considered overstatements. Check your printouts carefully to make sure your size variations have the intended impact.**

▶ **You can also change a selection's type size with the toolbar. Select the text you want to alter, and then click on the down arrow button at the left end of the toolbar, next to the narrow text box. A list box will drop down displaying the available sizes. Scroll to the size you want and click on it. Works will apply it to your selected text. If your selection contains more than one text size, the text and list boxes may be blank. Just type in the size, in points, of the text you want.**

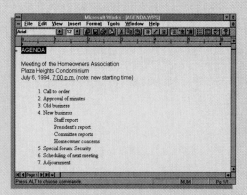

▶ **1** Type and select the text whose size you want to change. You can select any amount of text, from one character to an entire document.

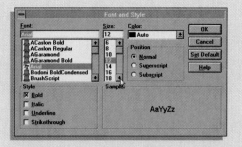

2 Click on Format in the menu bar and then click on the Font and Style command.

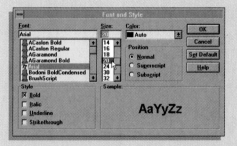

3 In the Size list at the top-center of the Font and Style dialog box locate the type size you need. You may have to scroll the list. The available type sizes depend on the font you are using and on the abilities of your printer.

Enlarged text

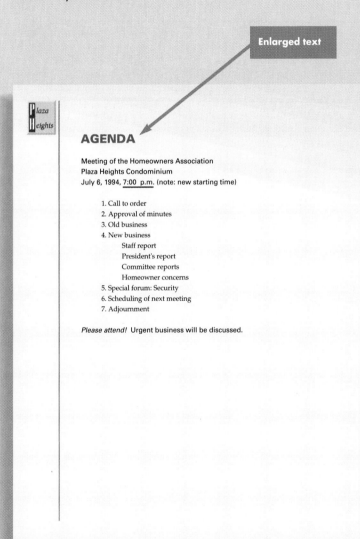

AGENDA

Meeting of the Homeowners Association
Plaza Heights Condominium
July 6, 1994, 7:00 p.m. (note: new starting time)

1. Call to order
2. Approval of minutes
3. Old business
4. New business
> Staff report
> President's report
> Committee reports
> Homeowner concerns
5. Special forum: Security
6. Scheduling of next meeting
7. Adjournment

Please attend! Urgent business will be discussed.

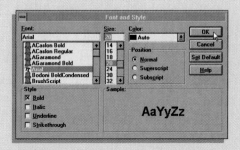

4 Click on the desired type size.

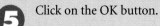

5 Click on the OK button.

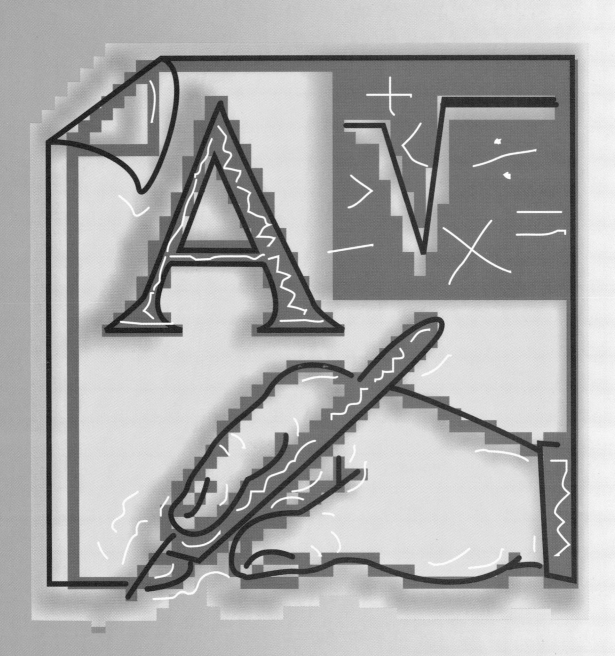

CHAPTER 7

Formatting

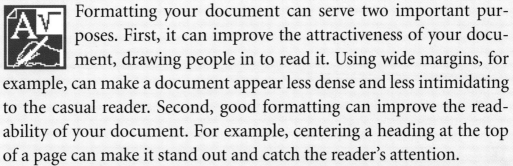Formatting your document can serve two important purposes. First, it can improve the attractiveness of your document, drawing people in to read it. Using wide margins, for example, can make a document appear less dense and less intimidating to the casual reader. Second, good formatting can improve the readability of your document. For example, centering a heading at the top of a page can make it stand out and catch the reader's attention.

This chapter covers two types of formatting: paragraph and page. *Paragraph formatting* affects your document on a paragraph-by-paragraph basis. For example, one paragraph may be single-spaced, and the next might be double-spaced. Line spacing, indents, and alignment are all forms of paragraph formatting. *Page formatting*, on the other hand, affects all of the pages of your document together. When you set the page margins, you do so for all of the pages in your document, and of course, all of the paragraphs on those pages.

How to Change the Line Spacing

L*ine spacing* is the amount of space between lines within a paragraph. In single-spaced text, there is no extra space between lines—just enough space so that letters don't overlap. Double-spaced text puts a blank line between lines of text. One-and-a-half spacing is a popular choice that makes text easier to read by separating lines of text with an extra half a line of blank space.

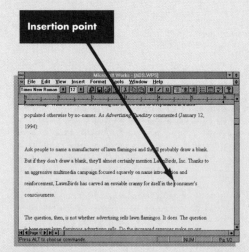

Insertion point

1 Place the insertion point anywhere in the paragraph whose line spacing you want to change. It can be a blank paragraph—one you have just started by pressing Enter. Alternatively, select adjacent paragraphs to specify the same line spacing for all of them.

TIP SHEET

▶ To change the line spacing for the whole document, click on Edit in the menu bar and then click on the Select All command. The whole document is selected. Then continue with step 2.

▶ You can enter any line spacing in the Between Lines text box. If the spacing you enter isn't a whole or half space, Works will convert it to points. (There are 72 points in an inch.)

▶ A new paragraph takes on the formatting of the preceding one. Therefore, if you are typing in a double-spaced paragraph and you press Enter to start a new paragraph, the new paragraph too will be double spaced. You can change the line spacing of the new paragraph—or of any paragraph—by following the steps on this page.

▶ In Works, any text leading up to a paragraph mark is considered a paragraph. A paragraph mark is placed in your document every time you press the Enter key. To see the paragraph marks in your documents, click on View in the menu bar, and then click on All Characters in the drop-down menu. This will display all the hidden characters that Works uses to format your documents.

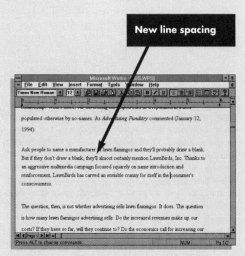

New line spacing

6 The new line spacing is applied to the paragraph or to all the selected paragraphs.

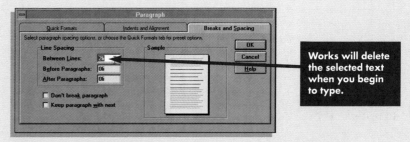

2 Click on Format in the menu bar and then click on the Paragraph command.

Works will delete the selected text when you begin to type.

3 At the top of the Paragraph dialog box, click on the Breaks and Spacing tab if it is not already active. In the Line Spacing group, double-click in the Between Lines text box to highlight all the text inside it.

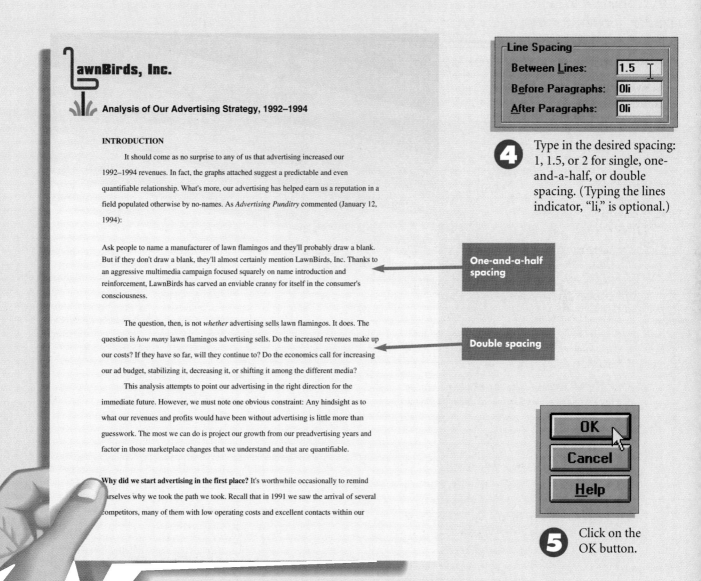

Line Spacing

Between Lines: 1.5

Before Paragraphs: 0li

After Paragraphs: 0li

4 Type in the desired spacing: 1, 1.5, or 2 for single, one-and-a-half, or double spacing. (Typing the lines indicator, "li," is optional.)

One-and-a-half spacing

Double spacing

OK

Cancel

Help

5 Click on the OK button.

How to Indent a Paragraph

Indentation is an effective way to call attention to a paragraph. It is also occasionally required by convention. For example, long quotations are by convention indented from the left (see the one in the sample document on this page). Microsoft Works lets you indent from the right, the left, or both.

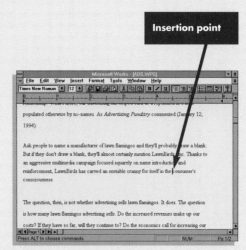

Insertion point

1 Place the insertion point anywhere in the paragraph you want to indent. It can be a blank paragraph—one you have just started by pressing Enter. Alternatively, select adjacent paragraphs to specify the same indentation for all of them.

▶ **To cancel indentation, repeat the steps shown here. In steps 3 and 4, specify indentations of 0.**

▶ **Microsoft Works measures indentation from the left or right margin (depending on whether you are assigning a left or right indent). Works uses default left and right margins of 1.25 inches each. So, for example, under the default margins, a left indent of 1 inch starts a paragraph 2.25 inches (1.25 inches for the margin, plus 1 inch for the indent) from the left edge of the paper. Indents remain the same relative to the margins. So, using the same example, if you change the left margin to 2 inches (explained later in this chapter), the paragraph will start 3 inches (2 inches for the margin, plus 1 inch for the indent) from the left edge of the paper.**

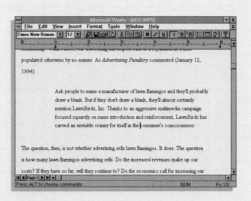

6 Works applies the indentation to the paragraph or to all of the selected paragraphs.

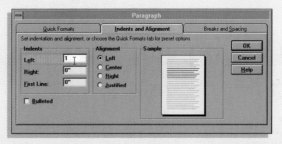

2 Click on Format in the menu bar, and then click on the Paragraph command.

3 At the top of the Paragraph dialog box, click on the Indents and Alignment tab if it is not already active. Then observe the Indents area. If you want to specify a left indent, double-click in the Left text box, and type the indent amount in inches. Typing the inch sign (") is optional.

Left indent

LawnBirds, Inc.

Analysis of Our Advertising Strategy, 1992–1994

INTRODUCTION

It should come as no surprise to any of us that advertising increased our 1992–1994 revenues. In fact, the graphs attached suggest a predictable and even quantifiable relationship. What's more, our advertising has helped earn us a reputation in a field populated otherwise by no-names. As *Advertising Punditry* commented (January 12, 1994):

> Ask people to name a manufacturer of lawn flamingos and they'll probably draw a blank. But if they don't draw a blank, they'll almost certainly mention LawnBirds, Inc. Thanks to an aggressive multimedia campaign focused squarely on name introduction and reinforcement, LawnBirds has carved an enviable cranny for itself in the consumer's consciousness.

The question, then, is not *whether* advertising sells lawn flamingos. It does. The question is *how many* lawn flamingos advertising sells. Do the increased revenues make up our costs? If they have so far, will they continue to? Do the economics call for increasing our ad budget, stabilizing it, decreasing it, or shifting it among the different media?

This analysis attempts to point our advertising in the right direction for the immediate future. However, we must note one obvious constraint: Any hindsight as to what our revenues and profits would have been without advertising is little more than guesswork. The most we can do is project our growth from our preadvertising years and factor in those marketplace changes that we understand and that are quantifiable.

Why did we start advertising in the first place? It's worthwhile occasionally to remind ourselves why we took the path we took. Recall that in 1991 we saw the arrival of several competitors, many of them with low operating costs and excellent contacts within our

4 If you want to specify a right indent, double-click in the Right text box to select all of the text in it. Type the indent amount in inches.

5 Click the OK button.

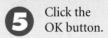

How to Change Paragraph Alignment

Alignment refers to the way each line in a paragraph interacts with the margins. Paragraphs of ordinary body text are typically either left-aligned (sometimes called "ragged-right"), like the paragraph you are reading now, or justified, which means that word-wrapped lines are stretched out with extra space to span from margin to margin, producing a squared-off look. Centering and right alignment are rarely used in ordinary paragraphs, but can be helpful in short paragraphs such as headlines. Notice that the sample document to the right includes right-aligned, centered, and justified paragraphs.

TIP SHEET

▶ Justification generally looks better with long lines than with short lines. With short lines, Works sometimes has to add extreme amounts of space between words to square-off the right margin. In a document that is otherwise justified, you may prefer to left-align heavily indented paragraphs or paragraphs typed in large type (because larger type produces correspondingly fewer characters per line). Notice that in this book, the chapter introductions—which have long lines—are justified, but narrower paragraphs—such as the one you are now reading—are left-aligned.

▶ Works treats all of its paragraph formatting as if it is stored in the paragraph marks. If you delete a paragraph mark, the preceding lines will take on the format of the next following paragraph mark. You can also copy formatting to your current paragraph by copying and pasting the paragraph mark of the paragraph you want to emulate. See the Tip Sheet under "How to Change the Line Spacing" in this chapter if you need help displaying paragraph marks.

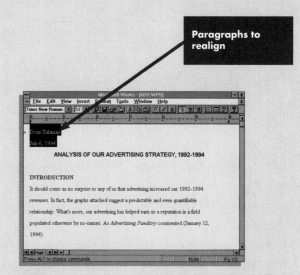

1 Place the insertion point anywhere in the paragraph whose alignment you want to change. Or, select any portion of adjacent paragraphs to specify the same alignment for all of them.

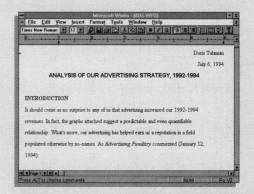

6 The selected alignment is applied to the paragraph or to all of the selected paragraphs.

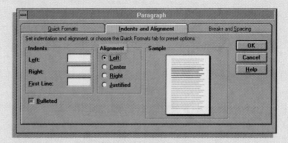

2 Click on Format in the menu bar, and then click on the Paragraph command.

3 At the top of the Paragraph dialog box, click on the Indents and Alignment tab if it is not already active. Locate the Alignment group near the center of the dialog box.

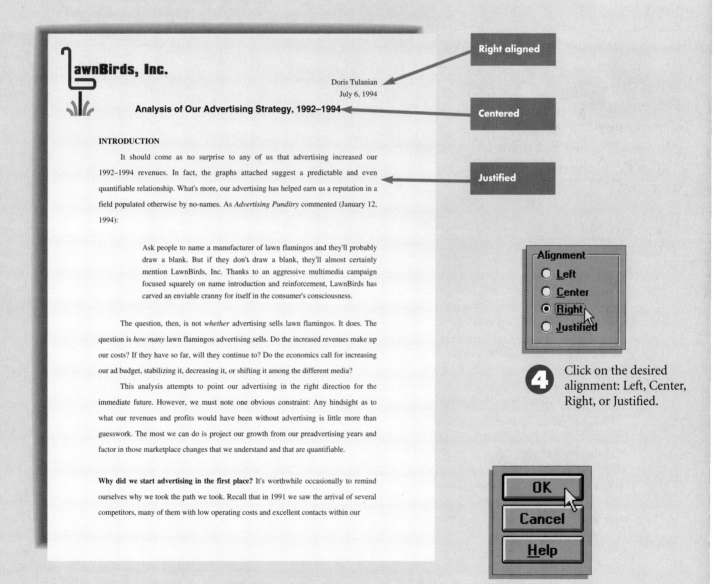

Right aligned

Centered

Justified

Alignment
- Left
- Center
- ◉ Right
- Justified

4 Click on the desired alignment: Left, Center, Right, or Justified.

OK
Cancel
Help

5 Click on the OK button.

How to Reset the Page Margins

Works uses default margins of 1 inch on the top and bottom of the page and 1.25 inches on the left and right. These margins are fine for most documents, but like all features in Works, they are by no means mandatory. Larger margins can give the page a gentler, more spacious feel, and (attention students) can increase the page count of a document. Narrower margins (attention résumé writers) can come in handy when you're trying to fit text onto one page. For example, in the document on this page, all the introductory text of a business report fits neatly on one page, and the report's author and date are tucked out of the way, thanks to customized margins.

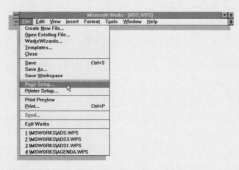

▶❶ Click on File in the menu bar and then click on the Page Setup command. (It does not matter where the insertion point is resting or whether text is selected.)

TIP SHEET

▶ Remember, in Microsoft Works, margins refer to the overall margins applied to every page. To change the margins of a paragraph or two, as in the second paragraph of the sample document on this page, use indentation as described earlier in this chapter.

▶ Because indents are added to margin settings, you occasionally get more than you bargained for. Let's say you assign a 1-inch left indent to a paragraph in a document with a 2-inch left margin. You get a whopping 3-inch indent with respect to the left edge of the page. Consider the effect of the margin setting when deciding whether and how much to indent a paragraph.

▶ Margin jargon can be slightly confusing. Note that "narrow" margins produce long lines of text, and "wide" margins produce short lines of text.

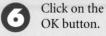 Click on the OK button.

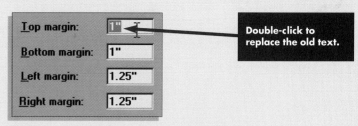

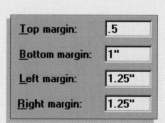

Double-click to replace the old text.

2 In the Page Setup dialog box, click on the Margins tab if it is not already active.

3 Double-click to select everything in the text box for the first margin you want to change: Top Margin, Bottom Margin, Left Margin, or Right Margin.

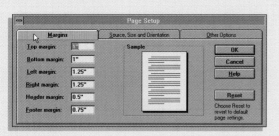

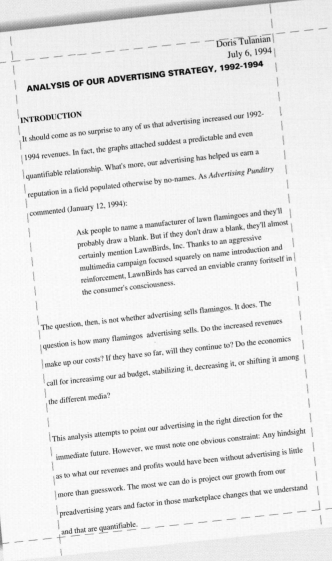

Doris Tulanian
July 6, 1994

ANALYSIS OF OUR ADVERTISING STRATEGY, 1992-1994

INTRODUCTION

It should come as no surprise to any of us that advertising increased our 1992-1994 revenues. In fact, the graphs attached suddest a predictable and even quantifiable relationship. What's more, our advertising has helped us earn a reputation in a field populated otherwise by no-names. As *Advertising Punditry* commented (January 12, 1994):

Ask people to name a manufacturer of lawn flamingoes and they'll probably draw a blank. But if they don't draw a blank, they'll almost certainly mention LawnBirds, Inc. Thanks to an aggressive multimedia campaign focused squarely on name introduction and reinforcement, LawnBirds has carved an enviable cranny foritself in the consumer's consciousness.

The question, then, is not whether advertising sells flamingos. It does. The question is how many flamingos advertising sells. Do the increased revenues make up our costs? If they have so far, will they continue to? Do the economics call for increasimg our ad budget, stabilizing it, decreasing it, or shifting it among the different media?

This analysis attempts to point our advertising in the right direction for the immediate future. However, we must note one obvious constraint: Any hindsight as to what our revenues and profits would have been without advertising is little more than guesswork. The most we can do is project our growth from our preadvertising years and factor in those marketplace changes that we understand and that are quantifiable.

4 Type in a new margin setting in inches. (Typing the inch symbol is optional.)

5 Repeat steps 3 and 4 for any other margins you want to reset.

TRY IT!

ere is an opportunity to try out the many skills you have learned in the first seven chapters of this book. Follow these steps to type, format, and print the document pictured here. Chapter numbers are included in italics to help you find more information on the skills required. Don't worry if your font looks different from the one shown here or if your lines break in different places. Factors like these can vary from one computer and printer to the next.

If necessary, switch on your computer, start Windows, start Microsoft Works, and click on the Start Works Now button to move past the Welcome to Microsoft Works screen if it appears. *Chapters 2–3*

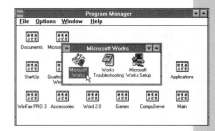

Marcie:

Memo

I've been looking into the grand opening celebration for the newest franchise in Anaheim. I just got off the phone with the caterer, and I'm really excited about the possible specialty snack foods. With the help of the existing restaurant, they can create and package any of our foods in snack-sized servings. *Take a look at this:*

Bite-sized Speedway burgers

Mini-orders of Speedway fries with our packaging

Speedway chicken tenders and

Speedway wings served in mini disposable foam automobiles

This is going to be the grandest opening yet!

Bruce

2

In the Startup dialog box, click on the Word Processor button to create a new word processor document. *Chapter 4*

3

Type the text of the memo. Don't worry about any of the formatting yet. Press Enter once to end a short line, twice to skip a line. *Chapter 4*

4

Select the last full sentence in the main paragraph (*This is going…*). Be sure to select the space after the exclamation point. *Chapter 5*

5

Click and hold down the mouse button on the selected text and drag it down to the line before *Bruce*. Release the mouse button. *Chapter 5*

6

Place blank lines both before and after this new paragraph. To do this, click at the beginning of each of the last two lines (*This is going…* and *Bruce*) and press Enter.

7

Select the text *Take a look at this:* at the end of the first main paragraph. *Chapter 5*

8

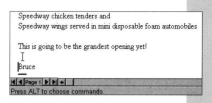

Click on Format in the menu bar, then on Font and Style in the Format pull-down menu. *Chapter 6*

9

Click on the Italic check box to select it, and then click on the OK button. *Chapter 6*

10

Select the text, *Memo*, at the top of the page. *Chapter 5*

Continue to next page ▶

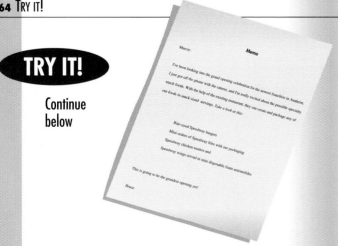

TRY IT!

Continue below

Click on Format in the menu bar, then on Font and Style in the Format pull-down menu. *Chapter 6*

Click on the Bold check box to select it. *Chapter 6*

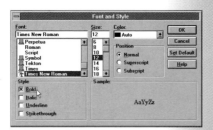

With the Font and Style dialog box still open, click once on Arial in the Font list box. You may have to use the scroll bar to find it. *Chapter 6*

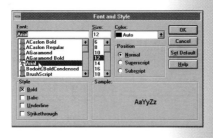

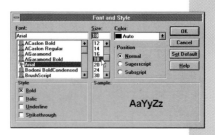

With the Font and Style dialog box still open, click once on *18* in the Size list box. You may have to use the scroll bar to find it. *Chapter 6*

Click on the OK button to close the dialog box and make all of the changes you have selected.

With *Memo* still selected, click on Format in the menu bar, then on Paragraph. In the Paragraph dialog box, click on the Indents and Alignment tab to activate it. *Chapter 7*

Click on the Center option button, and then click on OK to center this heading on the page. *Chapter 7*

Select the four lines starting *Bite-sized....* Click on Format in the menu bar, and then click on Paragraph. The Indents and Alignment tab should still be active. *Chapter 7*

19

Double-click in the Left text box under Indents and type the number **1**. Click on OK to indent these four lines 1 inch from the left margin. *Chapter 7*

20

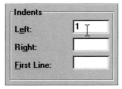

Click on Edit in the menu bar, and then click on Select All to highlight the entire document.

21

Click on Format in the menu bar, and then click on Paragraph. In the Paragraph dialog box, click on the Breaks and Spacing tab to activate it. Click anywhere in the document to deselect the text. *Chapter 7*

22

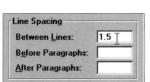

Double-click on the Between Lines text box and type the number 1.5. Click on OK to close the dialog box and one-and-a-half-space your entire document. *Chapter 7*

23

Click on File in the menu bar, then on Page Setup. In the dialog box, click on the Margins tab to activate it. *Chapter 7*

24

Double-click in the Top Margin text box and type the number .5. Click on OK to create a narrow top margin to prominently display the word *Memo. Chapter 7*

25

Click on the Save button to save your document. If you have not already saved it, type a name, like *cater*, in the File Name text box. Click on OK to save the memo. *Chapter 4*

26

Click on the Print button to print the new memo. It should appear on paper just as it does on your screen. *Chapter 4*

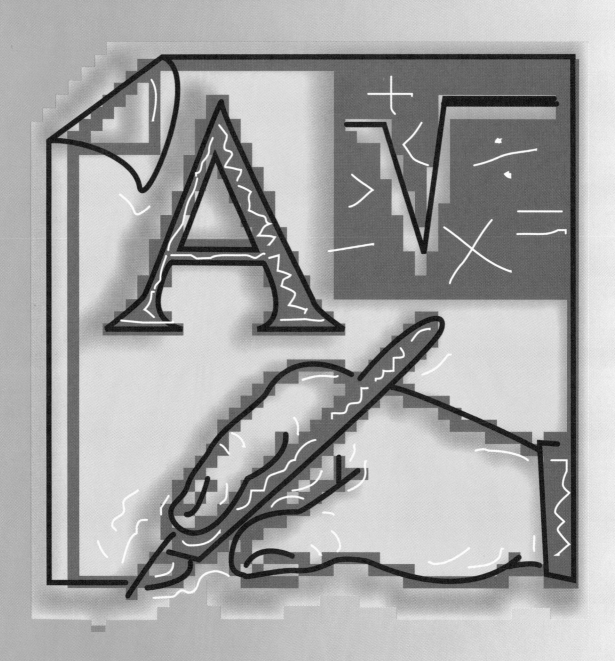

CHAPTER 8

Creating a Spreadsheet

 A spreadsheet is a table of *cells*, laid out in rows and columns on your computer screen. Each cell is a rectangle where you can type in a number, a text label, or a mathematical formula. "315," "March 15," and "=3*15" are all valid cell entries. (In Works, formulas don't end with "=," they begin with it—but you'll learn more about formulas in the next chapter.)

A spreadsheet program can help you perform repetitive calculations quickly, easily, and accurately. It can also let you check and change all of the numbers you've used in a calculation, even after showing you the result. A calculator, on the other hand, doesn't let you see all of the numbers you've used and lets you change only the last number you enter.

A spreadsheet program keeps all of the numbers, text, and formulas you enter in the computer's memory and displays them all on the screen so that it's easy to see them and understand how they're related. It performs calculations without error, showing you the numbers that went into the calculation, the numbers that came out, and the labels you chose to help you keep track of what all the numbers mean. It even lets you format everything you've entered to create professional-looking reports. If this sounds to you like a useful tool, it is. When most people learn how to use spreadsheets, they soon wonder how they ever got along without them.

How to Open a New Spreadsheet Document

The word "spreadsheet" can be used to mean a computer document for performing calculations, or it can mean the program that creates those documents. Either meaning will be commonly understood, but for the purposes of this book, "spreadsheet" will mean the document.

To learn about spreadsheets, the first step is to open one. When you do, you'll see a grid of lines partitioning the document window into short, wide rectangles. Each of these rectangles is a cell, a place to store data. You'll learn more about cells in the next chapter, but for now, take care of the first things first.

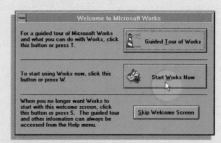

1 Start Works if you haven't already done so by double-clicking on the Microsoft Works icon in the Program Manager. If you see the Welcome to Microsoft Works dialog box, click on the Start Works Now button.

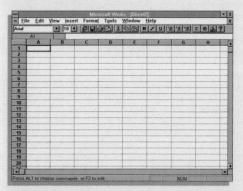

5 With your second document window opened and maximized, your screen should look like this. Notice that the new document is named *Sheet2*, since it is the second new spreadsheet document opened in this session of Works.

4 Once you've created one document, try creating another. Just click on the Startup Dialog button in the toolbar, and the Startup dialog box will open without affecting your first document. Click on the Spreadsheet button again to create the spreadsheet.

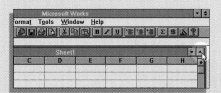

2 In the Startup dialog box you'll see that the New & Recent Documents button in the upper-left corner is depressed. When this button is depressed (the default), you'll also see a group of four square buttons across the right-center of the dialog box. This group is named "Create a new." Click the square Spreadsheet button to create a new spreadsheet document.

3 For a few extra cells in which to work, maximize the document window that appears inside the Microsoft Works application window. If the Microsoft Works application window isn't already maximized, maximize it, too. In the Microsoft Works title bar, you can see the current name of the new spreadsheet, *Sheet1*.

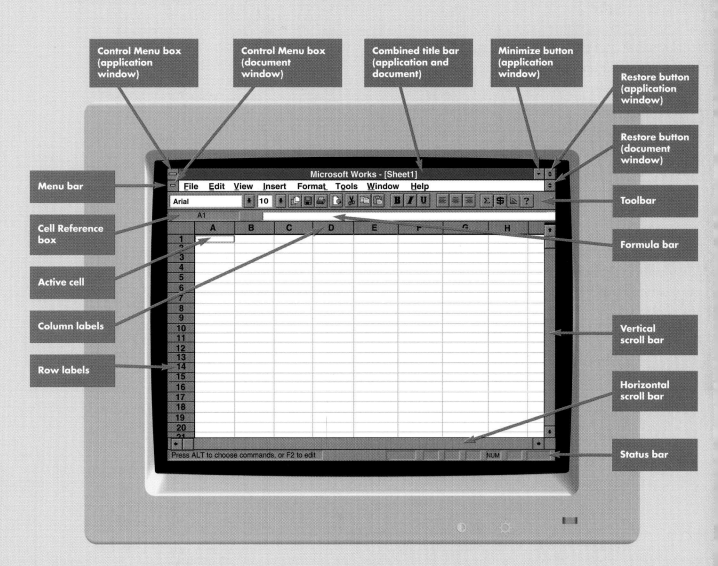

How to Enter Information into a Spreadsheet Cell

When you open a spreadsheet, you see a grid of lines partitioning the document window into short, wide rectangles. Each of these rectangles is a cell, a place to store data. You can store entire paragraphs in each of the cells (you won't be able to read them all at once, of course), but usually you'll use those cells to store the numbers that you need to perform calculations.

To help you tell the cells apart, each one has an address: a column letter followed by a row number. The first cell in a spreadsheet is always cell A1. That's just saying that it's the first cell in column A. The cell to its right is cell B1. Below that is cell B2.

Once you select a cell, there are two steps to entering information into it. First, you type data into the *Formula bar*, which serves as a temporary holding place. Next, you must tell Works to enter it into the cell, replacing what was there previously.

TIP SHEET

▶ Works will let you type up to 255 characters into any cell, but it doesn't try to display all the text in a cell. If you type a lot of text into a cell, Works will display it across the empty cells to the right. If you type in a very long number, Works will display it in scientific notation, "1E+10," or as a string of pound signs, "########," depending on the cell's number format (formatting numbers is covered in Chapter 11).

▶ When you begin entering text into a cell, two buttons appear in the Formula bar. The button with an X is the Cancel button. Clicking this works just like pressing the Escape key. The button with a check mark is the Enter button. Clicking this works just like pressing the Enter key.

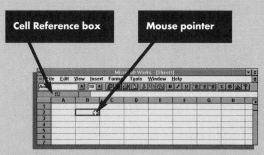

Cell Reference box | Mouse pointer

▶ **1** Choose a cell near the top of the spreadsheet and click on it. You'll see that the cell's address appears at the left end of the Formula bar in the Cell Reference box.

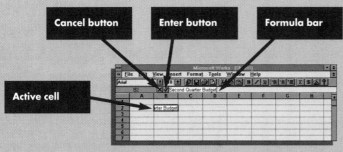

Cancel button   Enter button   Formula bar

Active cell

2 Type in text, in this case, the title of a table. As you begin, you'll see your text appear in two places: the Formula bar and the active cell (even though it isn't actually stored in the cell yet).

3 If you make a mistake typing, erase it with the Backspace key and retype the text.

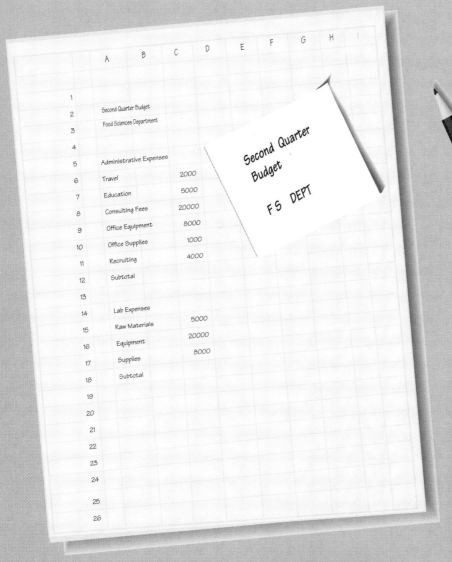

5 To cancel what you just typed and keep the cell's previous contents, press Esc.

4 To store in the cell what you have typed into the Formula bar, press the Enter key or click on another cell.

How to Select Cells

Selecting cells is much like selecting text in the word processor. By selecting a group of cells you mark it for an action, like entering data in sequential cells, deleting data, copying it, formatting it, and so on. You've already selected a single cell by clicking on it. Now, selecting cells in blocks will let you work on all of them simultaneously, saving you time and effort.

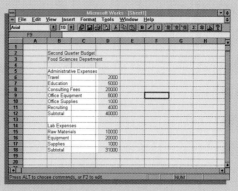

1 Locate the cells you want to select. If possible, scroll the document so that the entire block to be selected is in view.

TIP SHEET

▶ When you select a block of cells, all of the cells in the block except one are black. The one white cell is the *active cell*. It is the first cell you clicked on when you dragged to select the block.

▶ To select cells using the keyboard, first use the arrow keys to move to the cell at one corner of the block. Then, hold down the Shift key and use the arrow keys to move toward the opposite corner of the block, highlighting cells as you go. Release the Shift key when the complete block is selected.

▶ To select a complete row of cells, click on the row label on the left side of the spreadsheet.

▶ To select a complete column of cells, click on the column label at the top of the spreadsheet.

▶ To unselect a block of cells without performing an action on it, click anywhere outside the selection (but still in the spreadsheet). Or, if you're using the keyboard, release the Shift key and then press any arrow key.

5 Release the mouse button. The cells remain selected. Now you can issue commands that affect only the cells in this block.

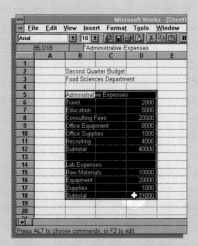

2 Position the mouse pointer at one corner of the block.

3 Holding down the left mouse button, drag the mouse toward the opposite corner of the block. As you drag over cells, they become highlighted, indicating that they are selected.

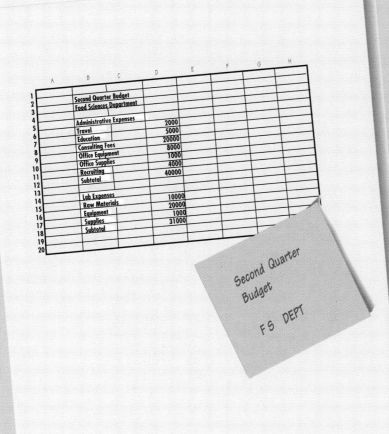

4 If you select too many cells, drag in the other direction to unselect them.

How to Enter Blocks of Information into a Spreadsheet

When putting together a spreadsheet, you'll often want to enter data into sequential cells. Entering data in one cell, then selecting the next, can be time-consuming. You have to move back and forth between the keyboard and either the mouse or arrow buttons, stopping to check your hand position with every move. To streamline the data-entry procedure, Works lets you select a block of cells and then enter data into those cells sequentially, without ever leaving the keyboard. This one-stop process makes typing data into a spreadsheet as efficient as typing in a word processor.

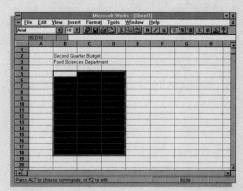

1 Start by selecting the block of cells that you want to enter information into. In this case, drag from the upper-left corner to the lower-right corner of the block. You'll select the block and leave the upper-left cell active, or ready to receive data.

Press Tab to move the active cell to the next column.

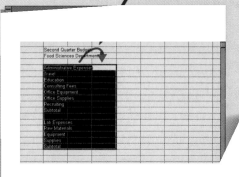

5 To move the active cell horizon across the block instead of verti press the Tab key instead of the key. You'll enter your data in the currently active cell, and move the active cell one cell to the right instead of one cell down.

TIP SHEET

▶ **The Enter and Tab keys move you to an adjacent cell *only* if you have a block selected. Make sure you do before you try to use them. If you don't have a block selected, you'll just replace the information in your currently active cell.**

▶ **The Enter and Tab keys move you down and to the right across a selected block. To move up and to the left, hold down the Shift key as you press Enter and Tab.**

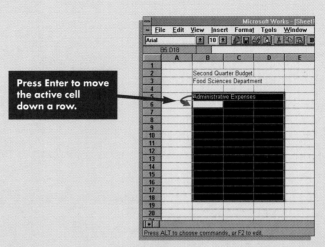

Press Enter to move the active cell down a row.

2 Type text into the upper-left cell as if it were the only cell selected.

3 Press Enter. You'll enter your new data in that cell and make the next cell in the column active.

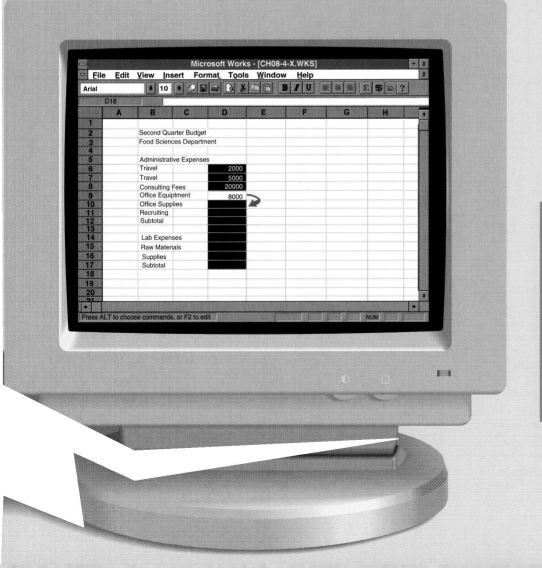

Press Enter to move the active cell to the top of the next column.

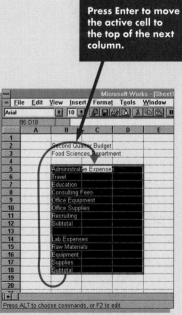

4 Continue entering data in this fashion. When you reach the end of a column of highlighted cells, press Enter to move the active cell to the top of the next column.

How to Save a Spreadsheet

As you work on a spreadsheet, it is temporarily stored in your computer's memory, or RAM, just like a word processor document. And just as you did with your word processor document, you need to save your spreadsheet to your hard disk when you exit Works or turn off your computer.

It's a good idea to save your spreadsheet (or any document for that matter) just after you create it. Then, as you work on it, save it every few minutes. That way you won't lose much work if the unthinkable happens and your computer malfunctions before you can save.

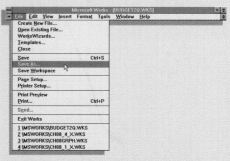

1 The easiest way to save a spreadsheet is to click on the Save button on the toolbar.

5 If you want to rename a spreadsheet after saving it, select the Save As command in the File menu. Works will open the Save As dialog box again so you can type in a new name.

4 To close your spreadsheet, double-click on the document Control Menu box.

TIP SHEET

- ▶ After you have saved a spreadsheet for the first time, you won't be asked to name it when you use the Save button again.

- ▶ Two alternatives to the Save button are to open the File menu and click on Save, or to press Ctrl+S.

- ▶ It's always a good idea to keep a backup copy of your work on a floppy disk. You never know when your hard drive might fail, or when someone may accidentally erase your file. To make a backup, select Save As from the File menu. Near the bottom of the dialog box, select your floppy drive from the Drives box. Click OK to back up your spreadsheet.

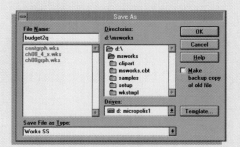

2 If this is the first time you're saving this spreadsheet, the Save As dialog box will open next. Click once in the File Name box in the upper-left corner of the dialog box, and type in a name of eight letters or fewer (no spaces or punctuation). Works will add the three-character extension .wks to the file name for you.

3 Click on the OK button. Your spreadsheet will be saved to your hard disk where you can retrieve it whenever you want.

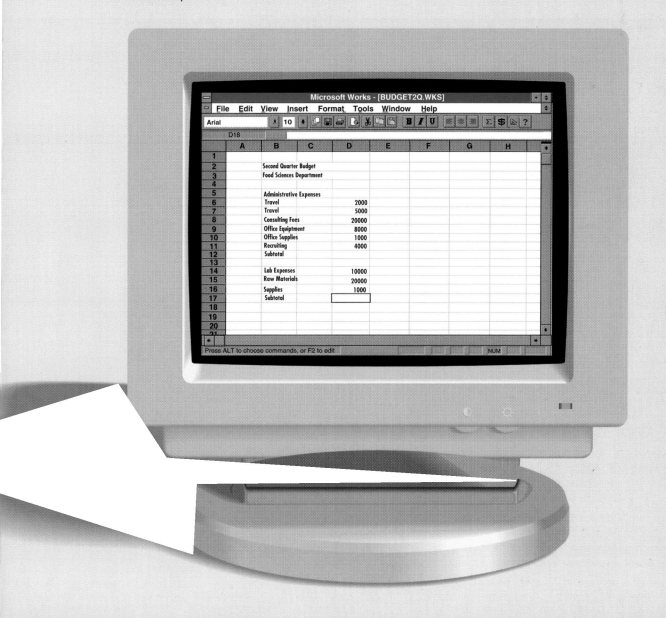

CHAPTER 9

Creating Formulas

 Formulas are simply mathematical calculations written in a way that Works can understand. Fortunately, you don't have to be a rocket scientist to enter formulas in Works. They look a lot like the arithmetic you've been using since grade school.

Formulas let you tell Works what math you want it to do. You might want to add up the cost of the items on your shopping list, or figure the gas mileage that your car is getting. You might even want to quantify the population changes in Alaskan caribou herds. You could do these things with a pocket calculator, but then you couldn't go back to make changes and correct mistakes. If you made a mistake with a calculator, you might not even know it. Formulas in Works let you make the calculations you want and see all the numbers that went into them. This way you can correct mistakes and change your assumptions as easily as entering new data into a cell.

How to Add, Subtract, Multiply, and Divide Numbers

Formulas perform mathematical calculations with numbers. When you enter a formula into a cell, Works calculates and displays the result in that cell. One example with two numbers is 987/3. In Works, you could write this formula in two ways: You could just type the equation into the cell preceded by an "=," or you could enter the two numbers in different cells, and then use their cell addresses in the formula instead of the numbers.

Using the first method gives compact spreadsheets capable of displaying large amounts of information on the screen at one time. Using the second method gives large sheets with easily accessible data. Either way, Works gives you the same answers.

TIP SHEET

▶ **Be sure to always enter your formulas according to standard rules of arithmetic. For example, Works won't know what to do if you put ** in the middle of your formula, or leave a + dangling at the end.**

▶ **Works ordinarily shows the results of your formulas in its spreadsheet cells. If you want to see the actual formulas displayed instead, click on the View menu then select Formulas.**

▶ **Whenever possible, arrange your spreadsheet so that similar items are grouped neatly together, and label your cells as if you won't remember what they are in 15 minutes. Later, you won't spend as much time figuring out what you did.**

▶ **If you're so inclined, Works lets you represent exponents with the ^ character and negative numbers by preceding them with a –. For example, Works reads =3*–1 as 3 times –1.**

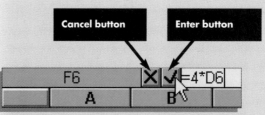

1 In Works, every formula begins with an "=." Click on a cell to select it and press =.

Cancel button   **Enter button**

6 When you are finished, press the Enter key or click the Enter button to store your formula in the current cell.

5 After you click on a cell, its address appears highlighted in the Formula bar. To keep the address, click on the Formula bar to the right of your equation to continue building the formula. To replace the address, click the cell whose address you want.

2 To include a number in your formula, simply type it in.

3 Type in the mathematical sign you want to use. Common math symbols Works uses are + (plus), – (minus), * (times), and / (divided by).

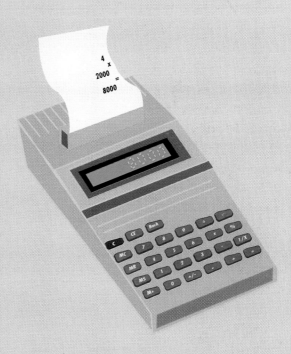

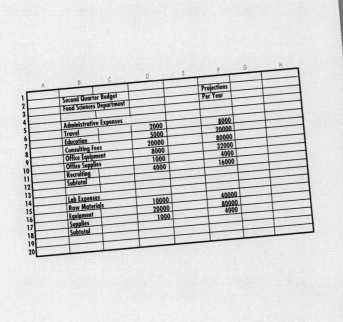

4 To include the contents of a cell in your calculation, click on the cell. Works will show the cell's address in your formula. Works accepts cell addresses in place of numbers in its formulas.

How to Sum a Column of Numbers

On the previous page you saw how to create mathematical formulas in spreadsheet cells. Suppose, however, that you had to total up several dozen items on a shopping list. If you tried to do this by clicking and adding each cell (=A1+A2+A3…), your mouse might need an oil change by the time you finished. What's more, it might be almost impossible to tell if you missed a cell.

Once again, Works has a solution to this dilemma: the SUM function. Beginners sometimes find functions a little hard to read at first, but they can make work so much easier and reliable that they will soon win your faith.

TIP SHEET

▶ In step 3 you saw a range of cells (D6:D11) in the Formula bar. This is the notation Works uses to describe blocks of cells. It consists of three parts: a starting cell address, a colon, and an ending cell address. The *starting cell* is always the upper-left cell in the selected block. The *ending cell* is always the lower-right cell in the selected block. You must use the colon to separate the two. You can type this notation directly into your formula if you like, but most people find using the mouse to be easier.

▶ Works has a few other functions to make working with blocks of cells easier: AVG calculates the mean or average value in a block. COUNT counts the number of non-blank cells in a block. MAX and MIN return the largest and smallest values in a block. STD and VAR calculate the standard deviation and variance of the values in a block.

▶ If you want to sum a column of numbers that doesn't contain any blank cells, try the Autosum tool on the toolbar. (It shows the Greek letter Σ.) Click in the cell just below the column you want to sum, and double-click on the Autosum tool in the toolbar.

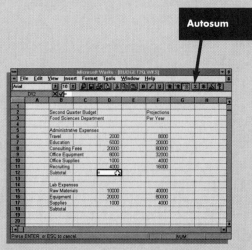

Autosum

▶ **1** To sum a column of numbers, start by clicking on a cell and typing an = sign.

3 Select the column of cells to add by clicking on the first cell and dragging down to the last cell. You'll see the *range* of cells you just selected appear highlighted in the Formula bar.

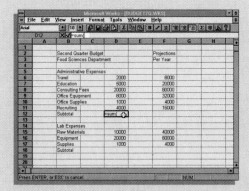

2 Type in the characters **sum(**.

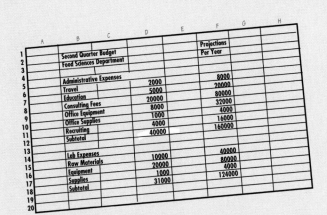

4 Type **)** to finish the formula and press Enter to place the new formula in the cell. Works will add all the cells in the block you selected and display the total in the cell containing the forumla. If you selected any blank or text cells, Works will count them as zero.

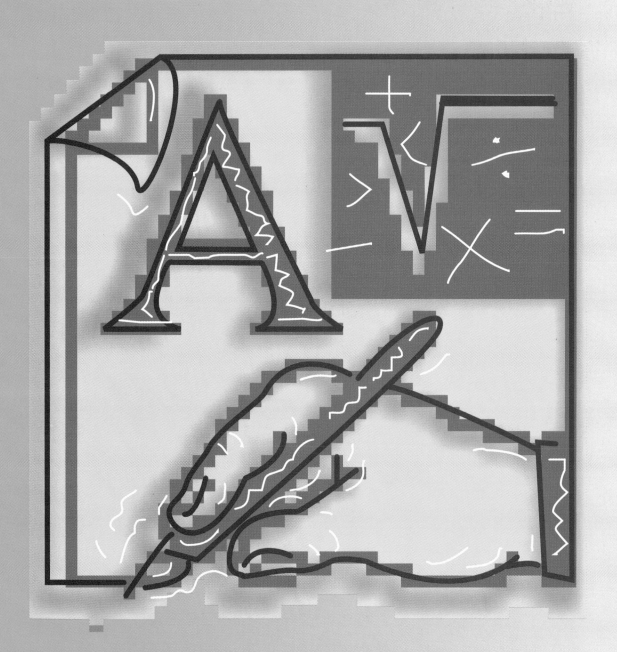

CHAPTER 10

Editing Cells in a Spreadsheet

You might want to edit your spreadsheet for any number of reasons. Maybe you entered a wrong number and need to correct it. Perhaps you want to modify the layout of your spreadsheet to accommodate new data or to display your data in a clearer fashion. In any case, Microsoft Works makes editing your spreadsheets as easy as editing your word processor documents.

In Chapter 5 you learned several techniques for editing word processor documents. Most of these have direct equivalents when you're editing spreadsheets. Navigation, insert and delete, copy and paste, drag and drop—Works brings all of these to the spreadsheet, slightly modified for working with cells instead of text.

How to Navigate to Another Part of a Spreadsheet

With one exception, navigating through a spreadsheet is much the same as navigating through a word processor document. The exception arises because spreadsheets can be dozens of times wider than the window you see on your computer screen. Not only do you have to navigate spreadsheets vertically, you also have to navigate them horizontally. Spreadsheets in Works can contain up to 16,384 rows and 256 columns.

As you might guess, the rows are numbered 1 through 16,384, but with only 26 letters in the alphabet, you may wonder how Works keeps track of so many columns. The answer is straightforward. The first 26 columns are named columns A–Z; the second 26, AA–AZ; the third 26, BA–BZ; and so on. Few Works users ever venture out beyond the standard alphabet, but it's nice to know that there's room to spread out if you ever get claustrophobic.

TIP SHEET

▶ **To navigate within the bounds of your past work, try the Home and End keys. The Home key will move the active cell and the spreadsheet view to column A in your current row. The End key will move you to the rightmost column in which you have worked.**

▶ **Press the Ctrl and Home keys together (Ctrl+Home) to move the active cell and the spreadsheet view to cell A1. Press Ctrl+End to move to the cell marking both the rightmost column and bottommost row in which you have worked.**

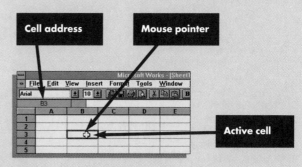

1 The easiest way to move the active cell is to point and click with the mouse.

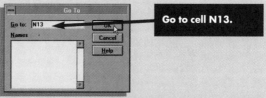

7 Type the cell address in the text box at the top of the Go To dialog box and click OK. Works will change the active cell to that address and will change the spreadsheet view to show it in the document window.

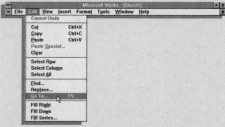

6 If you know the address of the cell you want to move to, use the Go To command. Click on Edit in the menu bar and then select Go To.

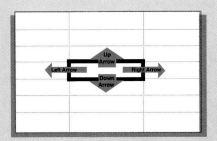

2 The arrow keys on the keyboard let you move the insertion point one cell in any direction.

3 The PgUp or PgDn key moves both the active cell and the spreadsheet view up or down by the amount you can see in the document window. Holding down the Ctrl key and then pressing the PgUp or PgDn key moves you respectively left or right by the amount you can see in the document window.

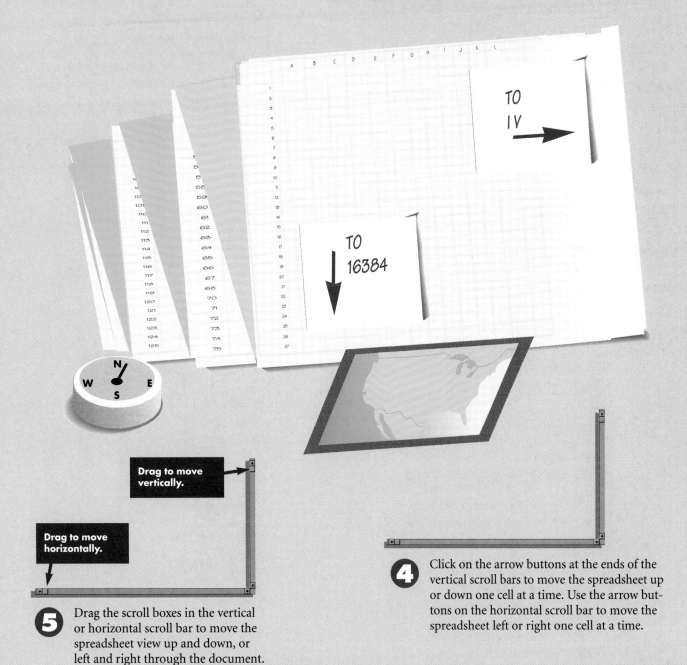

Drag to move vertically.

Drag to move horizontally.

5 Drag the scroll boxes in the vertical or horizontal scroll bar to move the spreadsheet view up and down, or left and right through the document.

4 Click on the arrow buttons at the ends of the vertical scroll bars to move the spreadsheet up or down one cell at a time. Use the arrow buttons on the horizontal scroll bar to move the spreadsheet left or right one cell at a time.

How to Move Cells

When working in spreadsheets, you'll frequently want to move the contents of cells from one location to another. You might do this to get old data out of the way of your new calculations, to bring numbers closer to the formulas that apply them, or to display information in a clearer and more concise fashion.

Moving cell contents brings up an important issue in addressing: What happens to the addresses contained in formulas that you move? As you might expect, Works doesn't change them.

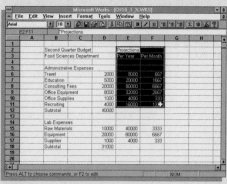

▶ **1** As with the word processor, drag and drop is the easiest way to move the contents of a small group of cells a short distance. To select the cells to move, click and drag to highlight them.

▶ **If drag and drop isn't working on your computer, you can turn it on in the Options dialog box. Click once on the Tools menu, and then select Options. Click near the lower-left corner of the Options dialog box to place a check mark on the Drag and Drop check box. Click on OK to close the dialog box and activate drag and drop.**

▶ **When pasting a block of cells, you needn't select the full destination block. It's easier to select only the upper-left cell instead. The cut block will overwrite the cells below and to the right of the single destination cell you choose. Be careful when you do this, since you can easily overwrite cells unintentionally.**

▶ **If you want to cancel a drag and drop after you begin, simply drag the destination outline back over the selected block of cells and release the mouse button. Work will drop them right where it picked them up.**

▶ **Whether you use cut and paste, or drag and drop, Works will move all the cell contents—text, numbers, formulas, and their formatting—to the destination.**

Ater the move, the formula still refers to cell D15.

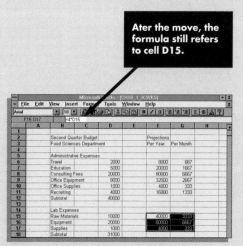

6 Select a block of cells for the destination—this must be the same size and shape as the cut block of cells. Open the Edit menu again, and this time select Paste. Works will leave the cut cells' contents in the destination block.

2 To move the cell contents, position the mouse pointer over the border of the selection so that it changes to the DRAG pointer.

3 Click the mouse button and drag the pointer to the desired location. As you drag, the pointer will change to read MOVE, and an outline of the selected cells will follow the pointer to show you their destination. Release the mouse button to place the cells in their new location

Destination outline

DRAG & DROP

5 Click on the Edit menu, and then the Cut command. Works will move the contents of the selected cells to the Windows Clipboard which, as you learned in Chapter 5, is a temporary holding place for data.

Before moving cell E15, the formula it contains refers to cell D15.

4 Cut and paste is the easiest way to move the contents of a large block of cells any distance, or any block of cells a long distance. To move a block of text using cut and paste, start by selecting the block of text to move.

How to Copy Cells

Copying cells is an easy way to fill out your spreadsheet. For example, you might want to repeat the same number several times. For saving time and improving accuracy, copying makes a lot of sense.

Copying *formulas* is another way to save time and improve accuracy. You might expect Works to treat addresses contained in formulas the same when *copying* formulas as it does when *moving* them, but this isn't the case. When you copy a formula from one part of a spreadsheet to another, Works treats the addresses as relative to the cell you copy. A *relative address* is an address relative to another address. For example, "the house next door" and "the cell to the left" are both relative addresses. They both relate the address to your current location.

Addresses in the formula tell Works to sum the numbers in the starting column.

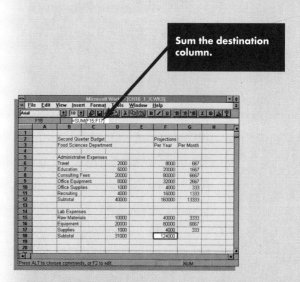

Sum the destination column.

▶ **1** Just as with moving cells, drag and drop is the easiest way to move a copy of a small group of cells a short distance. Use the mouse pointer to select the cells to copy.

 7 Select a block of cells for the destination. Open the Edit menu again, and this time select Paste. Works will copy the selected cells to the destination block.

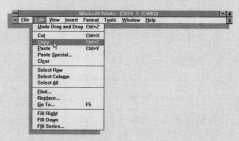

 6 Click on the Edit menu, and then select Copy. Works will copy the contents of the selected cells to the Windows Clipboard.

TIP SHEET

▶ **Works has a simple technique for copying the contents of one cell to many cells in a block. Copy the cell to the Clipboard as explained in step 5. Instead of selecting one cell as a destination as you would in step 7, select a block of cells. Works will paste the contents of the one cell you copied to all the cells of the destination block. This is especially useful for filling columns or rows with repeating data or formulas.**

▶ **After you paste cells from the Clipboard, a copy remains there allowing you to paste them again and again. Windows will leave the cells there until you perform a new Cut or Copy command.**

▶ **Whenever you copy text, be sure to examine the destination to make sure that all of the data and formulas transferred correctly, and that nothing important was overwritten.**

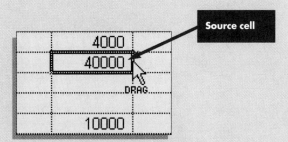

Source cell

2 To copy the cells' contents, position the mouse pointer over the border of the selection so that it changes to the DRAG pointer.

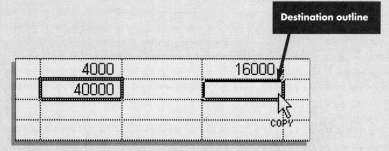

Destination outline

3 Hold down the Ctrl key on the keyboard, and then click and drag the mouse button. As you drag, the pointer will change to *COPY*, and an outline of the selected cells will follow the pointer to show you the destination.

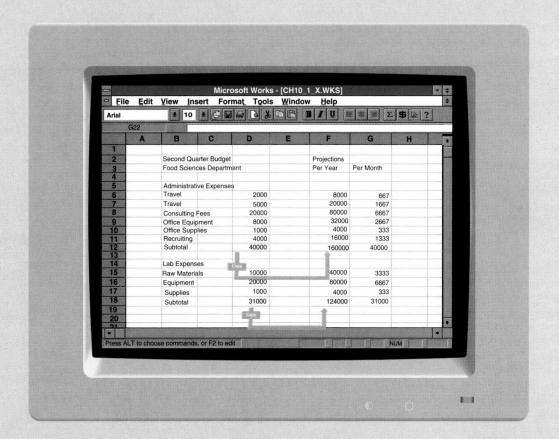

Addresses in the formula tell Works to sum the numbers in the destination column.

Sum the source column.

5 To copy the contents of any block of cells a long distance or a large block of cells at all, use copy and paste. Start by selecting cells to copy.

4 When you finish the copy, the addresses from the original column change to addresses in the destination column.

How to Remove Information from Cells

For some spreadsheet users, clearing cells can be like cleaning house. They keep unused or irrelevant data lying around their spreadsheets until they can't tell what's worth keeping and what's not.

The balance between showing too much on a spreadsheet and too little can be difficult to judge. When using a spreadsheet to perform complex calculations, it's generally best to delete information as soon as you know you won't need it again. Irrelevant data can easily be confused for the data you need to do your calculations. Of course, deleting formulas that you might need to justify your calculations might be going a little too far.

When using a spreadsheet for a presentation, it's generally best to show as little information as you can and still make your point. The simpler your spreadsheet appears, the easier it will be for your viewers to understand. If it looks too complex, it probably is. You might try breaking it down into two separate sheets.

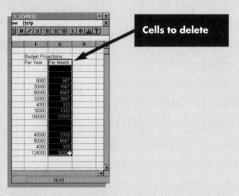

Cells to delete

1 To delete the contents of a single cell or a range of cells, select the cells with your mouse. When you select the cells, you'll be selecting all of their contents for deletion.

TIP SHEET

▸ You can also use the Delete key to empty cells of their contents. Simply select the cells you want to clear and press the Delete key.

▸ When you clear cells using the techniques described in this chapter, you clear them of text, numbers, and formulas. Number and text formats (covered in Chapter 11), however, are left behind and will affect any new data you put in the cells.

 Press Enter to keep the change you made to the cell. Press Esc to retain the cell's original contents.

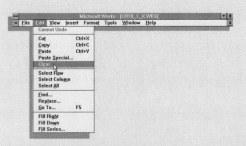

2 In the menu bar, click on Edit, and then select Clear. Works will remove the text, formulas, and numbers from all of the cells you selected.

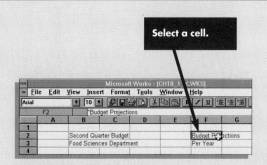

Select a cell.

3 To delete just a part of a cell's contents, start by selecting that cell.

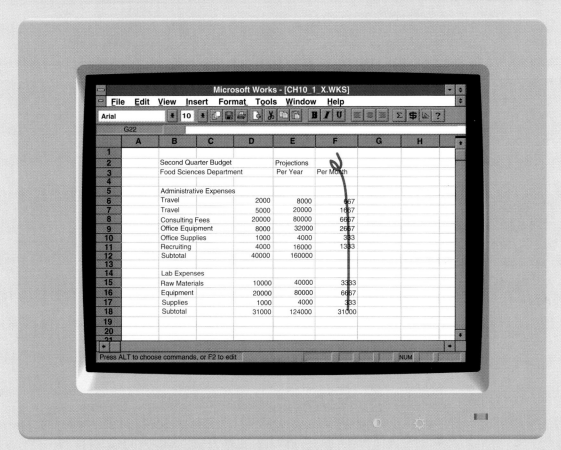

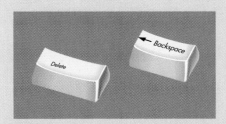

5 Press either the Backspace or Delete key to remove the selection from the Formula bar.

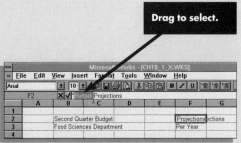

Drag to select.

4 In the Formula bar, click and drag with the mouse to select the portion of the cell's contents that you want to delete.

CHAPTER 11

Formatting and Printing a Spreadsheet

 There are no hard-and-fast rules when it comes to formatting a spreadsheet, but you should still keep in mind a few basic goals.

The first goal of formatting a spreadsheet is neatness. You want your reader to think you've been careful and thorough in your calculations, and displaying your information neatly will create a good first impression.

After the first impression, you need to communicate as much information as possible to your reader. While much of this task is the reader's responsibility, there are steps you can take to make that task easier. Organize your spreadsheet so that its results, or conclusions, are easy to find. The data supporting the conclusions should be easily locatable, but it needs to take a back seat to the conclusions.

Aside from demonstrating these general ideas, the best spreadsheets also have the following features: Using the table format presents data neatly and suggests relationships among entries. Clear and concise labels tell the reader what every piece of data is. Finally, simplicity makes your conclusions clear by reducing reader distraction—limit each table to one conclusion and its supporting data.

How to Format Numbers

Number formatting is the easiest, and often the most important, way to make your spreadsheet clearer and easier to understand. Microsoft Works has 12 basic options for formatting numbers. They range from displaying numbers as fractions, to scientific notation, to times and dates.

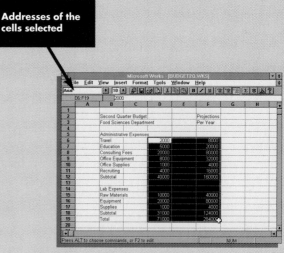

Addresses of the cells selected

1 Start by selecting the cell or cells containing the numbers you want to format. As usual, click and drag with the mouse to make a selection.

TIP SHEET

▶ If you apply a number format to an empty cell or to a cell containing a label, you won't see any changes there. If you later enter a number into the cell, however, Works will remember the number format and apply it to your new entry.

▶ The General format allows Works to guess what format you want based on the number you type in. For example, Works will display only as many decimal places as it needs to and will convert long numbers to scientific notation. Works will also judge whether a number is a special case, like a time, based on the format in which you type it.

▶ If you move or copy cells in a spreadsheet, you'll copy the number formats along with the cell contents.

▶ You can enhance the text in your spreadsheet just like you did in the word processor. The Font and Style dialog box in the spreadsheet is exactly the same as the one in the word processor, minus the options for superscript and subscript. (See Chapter 6 if you need help enhancing text.)

5 When you have finished making your formatting choices, click the OK button to apply them to your cell selection.

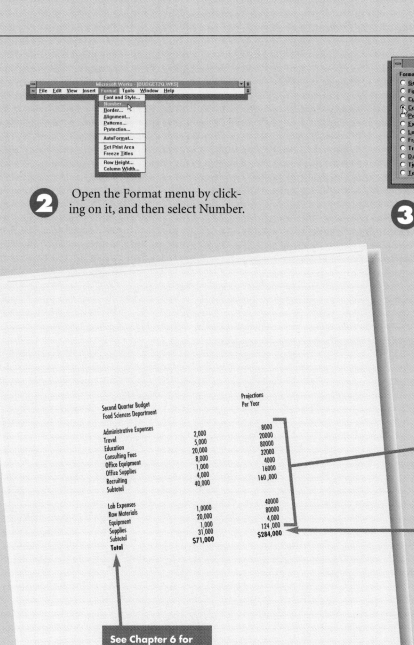

2 Open the Format menu by clicking on it, and then select Number.

3 In the Number dialog box, which opens next, click on one of the 12 formats. The sample at the bottom of the dialog box will change to reflect your selection.

Comma format

Currency format

See Chapter 6 for text enhancement.

Check to display negative numbers in red.

The zero instructs Works not to display any numbers to the right of the decimal point.

4 Most of the 12 formats have additional options that let you fine-tune them. In this case, the Comma format lets you select the number of digits you want to display to the right of the decimal point, and whether negative numbers should appear in red.

How to Align Items in Cells

The alignment of information within cells can help your reader pick information out of your spreadsheet quickly and easily by providing subtle clues as to what that information is. For example, titles are often centered over the cells they describe, numbers are usually aligned on the right so that their decimal points coincide, and text labels describing individual cells are usually aligned on the left, like lines of text on a page. Of course, you can stray from these informal conventions, but always keep in mind how your changes will affect the readability of your spreadsheet.

TIP SHEET

▶ **The General alignment option tells Works to guess what alignment you want based on the information you type in. For example, Works will left-align text labels and right-align numbers, dates, and times.**

▶ **The Fill alignment option tells Works to repeat the text in a cell to fill it from left to right. For example, you can create a simple border within your spreadsheet using a hyphen or asterisk with the Fill alignment option.**

▶ **The Wrap Text check box tells Works to break lines at the right edge of a cell to accommodate long text entries. The text will wrap to the next line, and the cell will automatically expand downward to fit it. This way, a long text label won't be covered up by the contents of the cell to the right.**

▶ **Besides fitting information to the cell that contains it, you can also change the cell to fit the information. To adjust column width to automatically fit the longest entry in the column, just double-click on the label at the top of the column (for example, A, B, C, and so on).**

Addresses of the cells selected

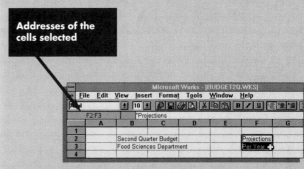

▶ **1** To set the alignment for a cell or group of cells, start by selecting the cells.

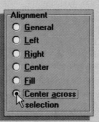

7 Follow steps 1 through 4 on this page. In step 3, select Center Across Selection in the Alignment dialog box.

6 Next, select the cells you want to center across.

2 Click on Format in the menu bar and select Alignment from the pull-down menu.

3 In the Alignment dialog box, click on one of the six option buttons on the left to select an alignment style for your cell selection.

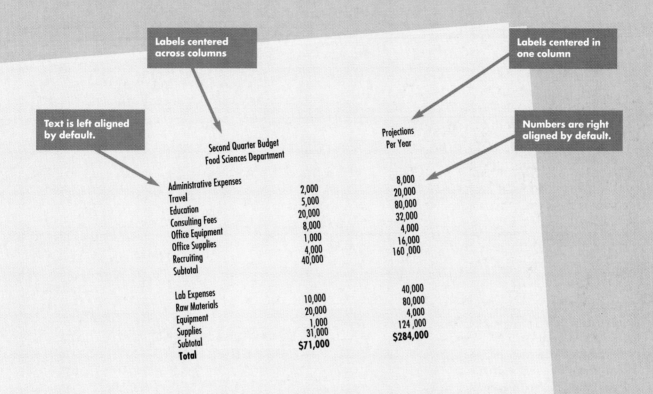

Labels centered across columns

Labels centered in one column

Text is left aligned by default.

Numbers are right aligned by default.

Second Quarter Budget
Food Sciences Department

Projections
Per Year

Administrative Expenses		8,000
Travel	2,000	20,000
Education	5,000	80,000
Consulting Fees	20,000	32,000
Office Equipment	8,000	4,000
Office Supplies	1,000	16,000
Recruiting	4,000	160,000
Subtotal	40,000	
Lab Expenses		40,000
Raw Materials	10,000	80,000
Equipment	20,000	4,000
Supplies	1,000	124,000
Subtotal	31,000	**$284,000**
Total	**$71,000**	

Labels are in the left column.

Columns to center across

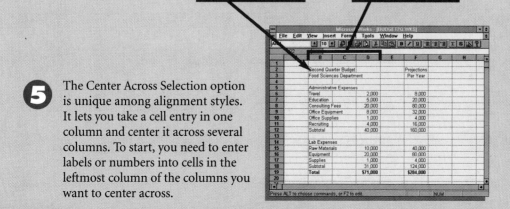

5 The Center Across Selection option is unique among alignment styles. It lets you take a cell entry in one column and center it across several columns. To start, you need to enter labels or numbers into cells in the leftmost column of the columns you want to center across.

4 Click on the OK button to align the items in the cells you selected.

How to Print a Spreadsheet

When you need to print your spreadsheet, maybe to impress the boss with your quantitative wizardry, maybe just to see all of your 15-page spreadsheet at one time, you'll find Works quite helpful. Printing spreadsheets is a little more complex than printing word processing documents, however, so you should know a few tricks to get just what you want.

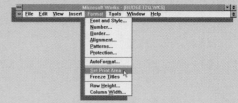

1 Works will print your entire spreadsheet by default. If you want to print just a portion of it, select the portion you want to print, and then select Set Print Area from the Format menu.

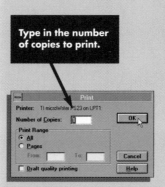

Type in the number of copies to print.

7 To send your spreadsheet to the printer, select Print in the File menu to open the Print dialog box. Then, type in the number of copies you want to print and click OK.

6 When you are through making selections in the Page Setup dialog box, click the OK button to apply your changes to the spreadsheet.

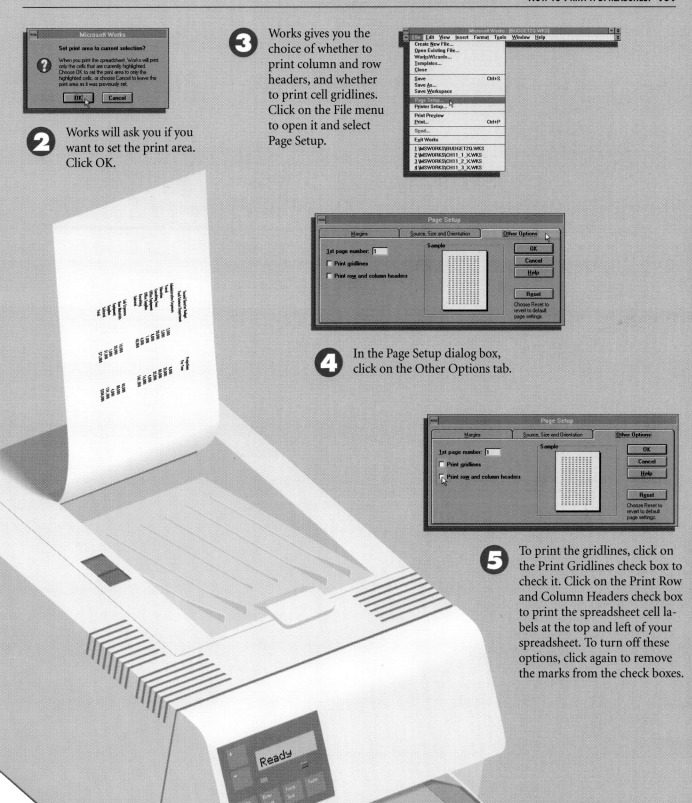

2 Works will ask you if you want to set the print area. Click OK.

3 Works gives you the choice of whether to print column and row headers, and whether to print cell gridlines. Click on the File menu to open it and select Page Setup.

4 In the Page Setup dialog box, click on the Other Options tab.

5 To print the gridlines, click on the Print Gridlines check box to check it. Click on the Print Row and Column Headers check box to print the spreadsheet cell labels at the top and left of your spreadsheet. To turn off these options, click again to remove the marks from the check boxes.

TRY IT!

In the last four chapters, you've assembled a solid collection of spreadsheet building and formatting techniques. Here is an opportunity to review these techniques and commit them to memory, so that you'll always have them when you need them. Follow these steps to create this simple spreadsheet. All of the steps include chapter numbers in italics to help you review information on the skills required.

Start Works, and in the Startup dialog box, click on the square Spreadsheet button to open a new spreadsheet. *Chapter 8*

Personal Summer Budget, 1994	July	August	September
Expenses	400	400	400
Rent	300	300	300
Car Payment	200	220	220
Groceries	150	150	150
School Loan	95	0	0
Insurance	75	0	0
Lunch at Work	20	20	20
Gasoline	100	100	100
Entertainment	200	200	200
Spending Cash			
	$1,540	$1,390	$1,390
Total	$1,750	$1,750	$1,900
Income			
	$210	$360	$510
Savings			

2

Maximize the document window by clicking on the Maximize button. *Chapter 8*

3

This spreadsheet is a personal budget. Enter the preliminary data shown here. You may want to select block B2:D17 before you begin. *Chapter 8*

4

Get in the habit of saving your work early and often. Click on the Save button. *Chapter 8*

5

In the Save As dialog box, enter the name **budget_3**. Works will assign the extension *.wks* to the file name for you. When you save your spreadsheet later, you won't have to enter the name again. *Chapter 8*

6

Click on cell D15, and double-click on the Autosum button in the toolbar. Works will write a formula in the cell to sum the column of numbers above. *Chapter 9*

7

Click on cell D17 and type the formula shown here into the formula bar. Press the Enter key on the keyboard when you are through. *Chapter 9*

8

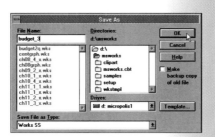

Move the contents of row 17 down so that the information will stand out more. Select cells B17 through D17 (B17:D17) by clicking and dragging. *Chapter 8*

9

Move the mouse pointer over the border of the selection so that it changes to the DRAG pointer. *Chapter 10*

10

Drag straight down one row. Release the mouse button to drop the cells. *Chapter 10*

Continue to next page ▶

TRY IT!

Continue below

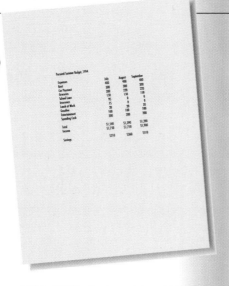

 11

Select cells D5:D18. Click on Edit in the menu bar, and select Copy. *Chapter 10*

12

Select the destination by clicking and dragging over cells E5:F18. *Chapter 8*

	A	B	C	D	E	F
1						
2		Personal Summer Budget, 1994				
3						
4		Expenses		July	August	September
5		Rent		400		
6		Car Payment		300		
7		Groceries		200		
8		School Loan		150		
9		Insurance		95		
10		Lunch at Work		75		
11		Gasoline		20		
12		Entertainment		100		
13		Spending Cash		200		
14		Miscellaneous				
15		Total Expenses		1540		
16		Income		1750		
17						
18		Savings		210		
19						

13

Click on Edit in the menu bar again, but this time select Paste. Works will copy the contents of column D to columns E and F simultaneously. *Chapter 10*

14

Suppose your finances change in the months of August and September. (You finish paying for your insurance, start carrying lunch to work, and get a well-deserved raise.) Change the data in columns E and F to reflect these changes as shown. Notice that the formulas at the bottom of the spreadsheet show new results. *Chapter 8*

	A	B	C	D	E	F
1						
2		Personal Summer Budget, 1994				
3						
4		Expenses		July	August	September
5		Rent		400	400	400
6		Car Payment		300	300	300
7		Groceries		200	220	220
8		School Loan		150	150	150
9		Insurance		95	0	0
10		Lunch at Work		75	0	0
11		Gasoline		20	20	20
12		Entertainment		100	100	100
13		Spending Cash		200	200	200
14		Miscellaneous				
15		Total Expenses		1540	1390	1390
16		Income		1750	1750	1900
17						
18		Savings		210	360	510
19						

15

Since there aren't any Miscellaneous expenses, clean up the spreadsheet by deleting the label. Click on cell B14 and press the Delete key. *Chapter 10*

B14			
	A	B	C
1			
2		Personal Summer Budget, 19	
3			
4		Expenses	
5		Rent	
6		Car Payment	
7		Groceries	
8		School Loan	
9		Insurance	
10		Lunch at Work	
11		Gasoline	
12		Entertainment	
13		Spending Cash	
14			
15		Total Expenses	
16		Income	
17			
18		Savings	
19			

16

Format the totals at the bottom of the sheet. Select cells D15:F18, and then select Number from the Format menu. *Chapter 11*

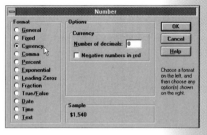

In the
Number dia-
log box, click
on the
Currency op-
tion button,
and set the number of decimal places
to zero before clicking OK. *Chapter 11*

To center the column la-
bels, select cells D4:F4.
Next, click on Format in
the menu bar and select Alignment.
Chapter 11

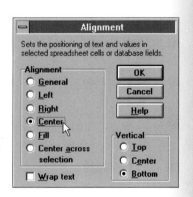

Select the
Center align-
ment option
button in the
dialog box,
and then click
OK to center
the labels.
Chapter 11

Save all of your work by clicking on the
Save button in the toolbar. *Chapter 8*

If you like,
print the
spreadsheet.
First, select
Print from
the File
menu. In the dialog box that opens next,
click OK. *Chapter 11*

CHAPTER 12

Creating a Database

 A database is simply any collection of information. It could be a Rolodex, a library card catalog, or a filing cabinet. It could even be a shoe box full of receipts.

In addition to stashing away information, databases perform several other functions. They make it easy to store information in a compact and organized manner. They make retrieval of the information within them fast and efficient. While a shoe box may perform some of these functions well, it might disappoint you if you had to store and dig through lots of information.

The database program in Microsoft Works performs all of these tasks well. Information storage is as easy as typing in text and can be as compact as a floppy disk. Just as important, information retrieval can be as easy as reading a name from a list.

Works also lets you apply the power of your computer to automate common uses of database information. You can create reports, or summaries, of your database's contents. You can even *merge*, or combine, the names and addresses in your databases with a word processor document to automate and personalize your next mailing. Don't try that with a shoe box.

How to Create a Form

The first step in creating a database is to create a form. A *form* is basically a template that you use to enter data into your database. For example, if you wanted to create a database of your friends' names and phone numbers, you would need to create a form with places to enter those two kinds of data.

After creating the form, the next step is to enter data using the form. People familiar with databases use two terms to describe that entered data: fields and records. *Fields* are individual pieces of data. *Records* are groups of data that are often used together. In the previous example, there would be two fields: Name and Phone Number. There would also be an unlimited number of records: one for each friend who likes you enough to give you his or her number.

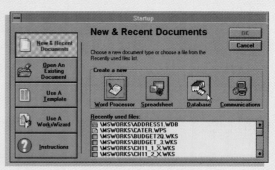

1 Start by creating a new database document. Start Works, and in the Startup dialog box, click on the square Database button.

Plaza Heights Residents

Name: _ _ _ _ _ _ _ _ _ _

Number: _ _ _

9000 Brush Street

San Francisco, CA 94109

Phone: _ _ _ _ _ _ _ _ _ _

Text labels appear only on the form.

Fields allow you to enter information into the database.

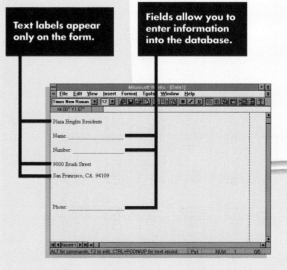

8 Click and type to add new text labels to the form. Repeat steps 4 through 7 to create and resize additional fields.

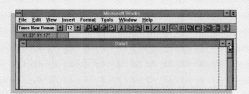

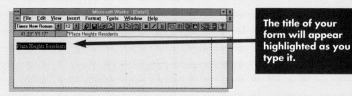

The title of your form will appear highlighted as you type it.

2 Maximize the document window by clicking on its Maximize button.

3 You'll see the insertion point blinking at the top of the window. Type a descriptive title that you want to see at the top of your form as you enter and retrieve data. Press Enter to place it on the form.

Plaza Heights Residents

Name:

Number:

9000 Brush Street

San Francisco, CA 94109

Phone:

Click to place a field.

4 Click to position the first field in your form.

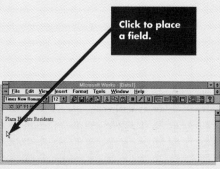

5 From the Insert menu, select Field. The Insert Field dialog box will appear.

Field name

Field box for typing information (names)

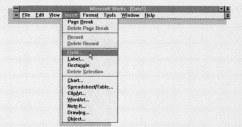

Drag a handle to resize a field box.

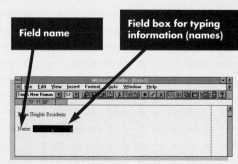

7 Click and drag the square handles on the field box to resize it. Drag to the left or right to adjust the box length, and up or down to adjust the number of rows. This will give you room for the information you enter into the field.

6 Type in the field name and click OK. The name will appear along with a rectangular field box on your form. Later, you'll use that box to enter information into the database for each record.

How to Enter Information with a Form

Once you have created a database form, you can begin to enter the data that you want to organize with your database. As you learned in the last section, the database form is simply a stencil for entering information. The field boxes are the openings in the stencil to enter that information. The information in all the fields on the form taken together makes up a record.

When you enter information using your form, you'll generally do so one record at a time. In this example, that means entering all the data for each person before moving on to the next record.

TIP SHEET

▶ **Form View is best when you're working with one record at a time and want to see the relationship between the fields. List View is good for viewing many records together and seeing the relationship between the records and field entries.**

▶ **To navigate from one record to another, use the navigation buttons at the bottom of the screen. From left to right, they move you to the first record, the previous record, the next record, and the last record.**

▶ **To find information in any record, use the Find command in the Edit menu. In the Find dialog box, type in the text or numbers you're looking for. Works will search for exact matches in all the fields of all the records in the database.**

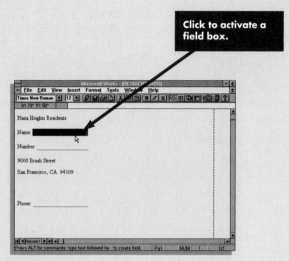

Click to activate a field box.

▶ **1** Open a database containing a form you've created. Click on the first field box to highlight and activate it.

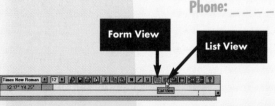

Plaza Heights Residents

Name: _ _ _ _ _ _ _ _ _ _

Number: _ _ _

9000 Brush Street

San Francisco, CA 94109

Phone: _ _ _ _ _ _ _ _ _ _

Form View   List View

6 After you have entered a few records, you might try switching to List View to see more than one record at a time. List View looks a lot like a spreadsheet with the records displayed in rows and the fields organized in columns. You can make this selection by selecting List from the View menu or by clicking on the List View button on the toolbar. To switch back to Form view, select Form from the View menu, or click on the Form View button on the toolbar, immediately to the left of the List View button.

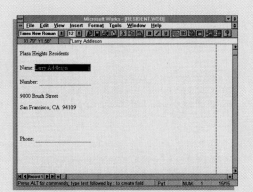

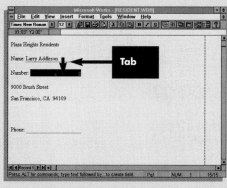

3 To store the data in the database and move to the next field, press Tab or click with the mouse on the next field. If you want to cancel without storing the data you've typed into a field, press Esc.

2 Type in the information that the field name asks for.

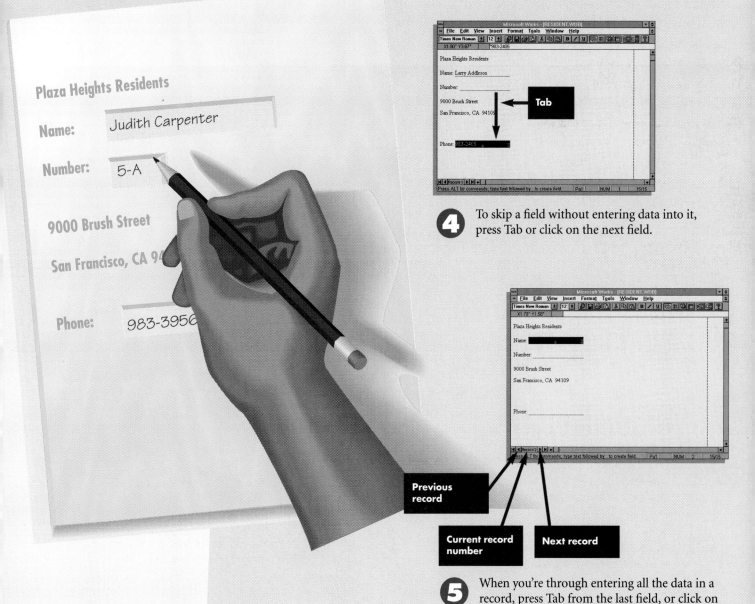

4 To skip a field without entering data into it, press Tab or click on the next field.

Previous record

Current record number

Next record

5 When you're through entering all the data in a record, press Tab from the last field, or click on the Next Record button after you press Enter to create a new blank record for your next data entry.

How to Edit a Database

Even if you have flawless information, errors will still find their way into your database. Friends move, contacts change, objects in your inventory grow legs and move to sunnier climes. Sooner or later, you'll need to modify the database you've worked hard to develop. When that time comes, you'll find some of the same techniques available that you used to edit the word processor and spreadsheet. Steps 1 through 3 here describe editing techniques in Form View; steps 4 through 6, editing techniques in List View. Finally, steps 7 and 8 describe general techniques for editing a database.

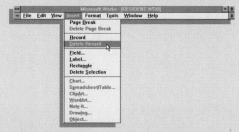

▶ **1** To delete a record in Form View, click anywhere in that record and choose the Delete Record command from the Insert menu.

Plaza Heights Residents

Daniel Davis

4-C

9000 Brush Street

San Francisco, CA 94109

1(415)983-4563

Click and type to update a field.

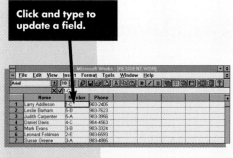

8 You can always overwrite the contents of a field. Simply click on the field box and type in new data. Press Enter when you are done to record your changes.

TIP SHEET

▶ **You can format the text in a database just as you would in a spreadsheet or word processor. Switch to the view that you want to modify, select the text, and use the formatting options on the toolbar or in the Format menu. Bear in mind that the formatting will apply across all records. That is, if you boldface a field name in one record, it will appear bold in all records.**

▶ **In List View you can adjust column width to fit the widest data a column contains. Double-click on the field name at the top of the column. Works will find the widest entry in the field and adjust the column width to show that entry (and all the others) clearly.**

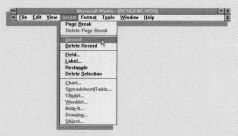

2 To insert a record in Form View, move to the record that will come after the new record, and then select Record in the Insert menu.

3 To remove a field from all the records while you're in Form View, first click on the field name (not the field box). Press the Delete key and select OK when Works asks you to confirm. Before you remove a field, make sure you don't need any of the data it contains. You cannot undo this operation.

4 To delete a record in List View, select any part of that record and choose the Delete Record/Field command from the Insert menu. In the Delete dialog box that follows, select Record and click OK.

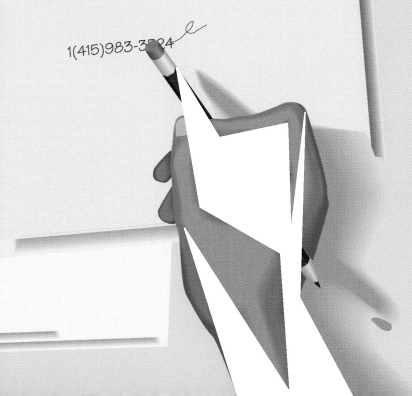

Plaza Heights Residents

Judith Carpenter

5-b

9000 Brush Street

San Francisco, CA 94109

1(415)983-3524

5 To remove a field from every record while you're in List View, click anywhere in the field and select the Delete Record/Field command from the Insert menu. In the Delete dialog box that follows, select Field and click OK. Again, make sure you don't need the data contained in the field, since you cannot undo this operation.

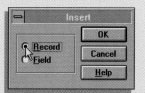

6 Insert a record in List View by selecting Record/Field from the Insert menu. In the Insert dialog box that follows, click the Record option button, and then click OK.

7 To delete the contents of a field, click on that field box and press Del.

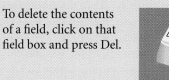

How to Print a Report

Reports are a convenient way to tabulate, summarize, and print the information in your database. They have four parts: title, column headings, records, and summaries. You specify the title that Works prints at the top of your report. You can also choose the column headings, but Works suggests the field names by default. As for the records, Works prints every record on its own line below the column headings, while the fields chosen for the column headings determine which fields appear on each line. Finally, you select what data summaries, or report statistics, you want Works to display for each field at the bottom of the report.

▶ **1** Open the database from which you want to create a report, and click on the Report View button on the toolbar.

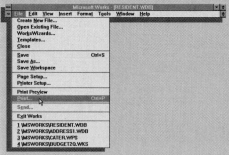

7 Print your report for a hard copy of all tabulated records and statistics. As usual, select Print from the File menu.

TIP SHEET

▶ To see your report without printing a hard copy, select Print Preview from the File menu. Works will create a mock-up of your document and display it on the screen.

▶ You can edit your report once you've created it. In Report View, click on and type over the title or headings to change them; or if you want, click on and delete fields and summary information with the Delete key.

▶ If you set your column widths in List View before generating a new report, the report columns will take on the sizes of the corresponding list columns.

▶ To set column width after your report is generated, move the mouse pointer over the border between column headings so that it changes to the ADJUST pointer. Click and drag the column border to find the ideal size, and then release the mouse button.

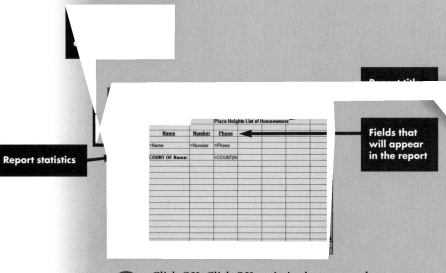

Report statistics

Fields that will appear in the report

6 Click OK. Click OK again in the message box telling you the report has been created. You'll generate a report outline without any data, but showing all of the selections you have made.

2 Type the report title at the top of the New Report dialog box.

Fields in the database

Fields included in the report

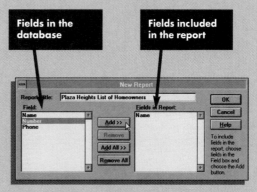

3 For each field that you want to appear as a column in the report, click on the field name, then on the Add button. When you are through, click the OK button.

4 In the Report Statistics dialog box, select the statistics you want to calculate. Click on a field, and then select the appropriate check boxes to the right for the statistics you want to see.

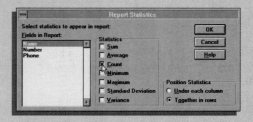

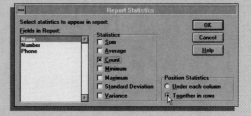

5 In the lower-right corner of the dialog box, click on one of the two option buttons to place the report statistics either under each column or together in rows at the bottom of the report.

CHAPTER 13

Creating a Mass Mailing

Are you intrigued by personal mail from people you've never met? Do you collect those little cards that fall out of magazines? If so, you're about to find your calling. You can stop waiting by the mailbox for the next clearinghouse giveaway and turn instead to creating your own mailings. With Works, you can turn out personal letters faster than your recipients can read them.

But, seriously, you may have a real need for mass mailings. Maybe you need to send bills to all of your customers with outstanding balances. Perhaps you just want revenge for all those photocopied holiday card inserts you received last year. No matter what your purpose, mass mailings can be a time- and cost-efficient method for delivering your message.

The key to creating a mass mailing is a technique called merging. *Merging* is simply the process of taking personal information from your database, one record at a time, and inserting it into your word processor document, one copy at a time. That way, you get one copy of your letter for each record in your database, each with its own database information. If you can create a letter and create a database, you're well on your way to merging the two for your next mailing.

How to Create a Form Letter

You learned in the previous chapter how to create a database for your mailing list. Once you complete your database, the next step in creating a mailing is to create the form letter.

Form letters are much like ordinary letters, but with one major difference: They have special placeholders for personal information instead of the real thing. *Placeholders* are word processor objects you insert in your document. They mark on each form letter the location where you want to print the contents of a database field.

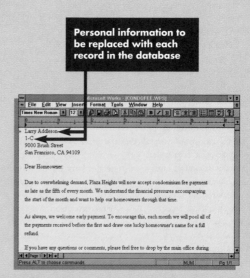

Personal information to be replaced with each record in the database

1 With the word processor, create, write, and save the letter you want to send to several people. Type in personal information as you go, just as a reminder of where you want to place the information in the database fields when you perform the merge.

▶ **You can create form letters of varying levels of sophistication by inserting different fields. For example, if you have separate database fields for a person's title, first name, and last name, you can generate a personalized greeting by combining those fields: Dear <<Title>> <<Last Name>>:**

▶ **You're not limited to address information when you merge. You can include any relevant information that you keep in your database. For example, you may want to send letters to all of your credit customers with outstanding balances. If you have created a database containing information about amount owed, you can insert a placeholder for that information into your document, and Works will merge the data in automatically at the same time as the address.**

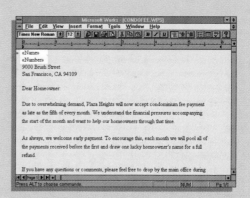

7 To insert additional fields, one by one, into your document, you'll need to repeat steps 2, 3, and 6. (If you repeat steps 4 and 5, you could end up selecting another database, which may not contain the information you need.)

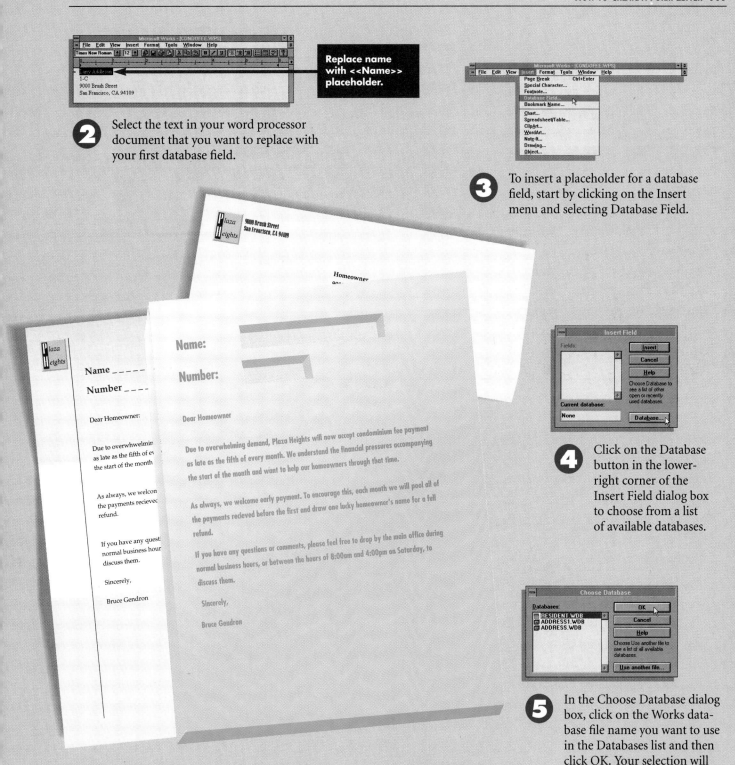

2 Select the text in your word processor document that you want to replace with your first database field.

Replace name with <<Name>> placeholder.

3 To insert a placeholder for a database field, start by clicking on the Insert menu and selecting Database Field.

4 Click on the Database button in the lower-right corner of the Insert Field dialog box to choose from a list of available databases.

5 In the Choose Database dialog box, click on the Works database file name you want to use in the Databases list and then click OK. Your selection will appear in the Current Database box when the Insert Field dialog box returns to your screen.

6 Click on the field name you want and then the Insert button. Works will replace the selected text in your word processor document with a placeholder for the database field, and the Cancel button will change to read "Close." Click the new Close button to return to your document.

How to Merge a Letter and a Mailing List

In the previous spread you learned how to prepare a word processor document to become a form letter. With the database ready, merging these two is the final step in creating your mailing.

Works performs your merge as part of the printing process. You've already used the Print command to output your documents, but taking just a few extra steps along the way will allow you to electronically generate a unique printout for each record, or person, in your database.

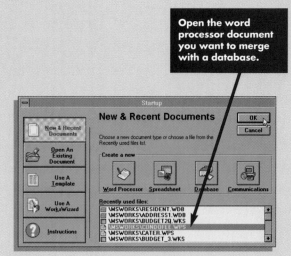

Open the word processor document you want to merge with a database.

▶ **1** Start Works if you haven't already done so, and open the word processor document that you want to merge. (To merge with a database, you'll need field placeholders in your document. See the previous spread if you need help with this.)

TIP SHEET

▶ Because print merges can use large quantities of paper, make sure you have everything in order before you begin printing. Check your document for spelling, grammar, and syntax, and check that you're merging the correct database.

▶ You can save paper by looking over your merged document before you print it. Instead of selecting Print in step 2, open the File menu and click on Print Preview. Skip step 3 and move on to steps 4 and 5. Works will merge your documents in memory and display them on your screen. Click the Next and Previous buttons to view the different copies of your letter. Click the Cancel button to return to your document.

▶ If you leave a field in your database blank, during the merge Works will treat it like it doesn't exist. If the field is on a line with other text, Works will close up the text around it. If the field is on a line by itself, Works will delete the line.

▶ When you merge the document with the database, make sure the font used for the field text matches the font used for the rest of the document. Any benefit gained from personalizing your document will be lost if it looks like a ransom note.

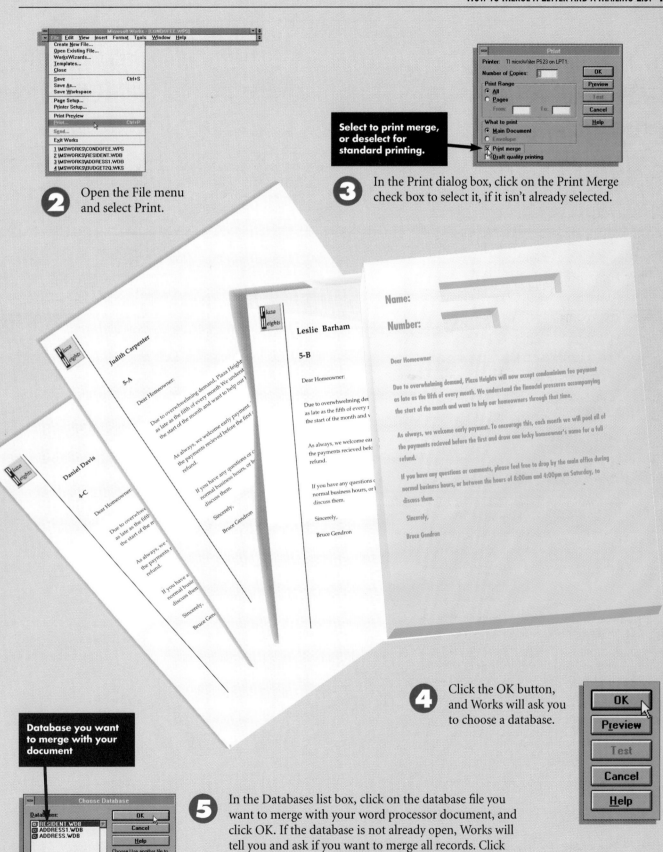

Select to print merge, or deselect for standard printing.

2 Open the File menu and select Print.

3 In the Print dialog box, click on the Print Merge check box to select it, if it isn't already selected.

4 Click the OK button, and Works will ask you to choose a database.

Database you want to merge with your document

5 In the Databases list box, click on the database file you want to merge with your word processor document, and click OK. If the database is not already open, Works will tell you and ask if you want to merge all records. Click the OK button. Works will print your document once for each record in the database.

How to Print the Mailing Labels

With your print merge finished, there are only a few tasks separating your stack of printouts and the post office. Works can't stuff the envelopes or lick the stamps, but it can automate the most tedious and time-consuming job remaining: printing the mailing labels.

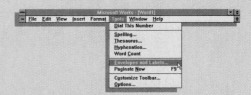

1 Open a new word processor document and select Envelopes and Labels from the Tools menu. In the Envelopes and Labels dialog box, select the Mailing Labels tab.

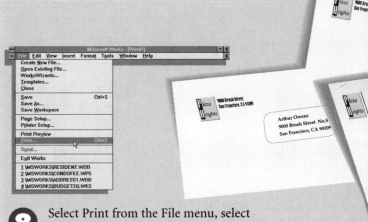

8 Select Print from the File menu, select the Print Merge check box, and click OK. Works will display the Choose Database dialog box, asking what database you want to merge with your new labels document. Click on the same database you chose in step 4, and then click OK. Click OK again when Works asks if you want to merge all the records in your database.

7 Click the Create Label button to close the Envelopes and Labels dialog box and create a label at the top of your document window. The label format you chose in step 2 includes all the margin and spacing information Works needs to generate full sheets.

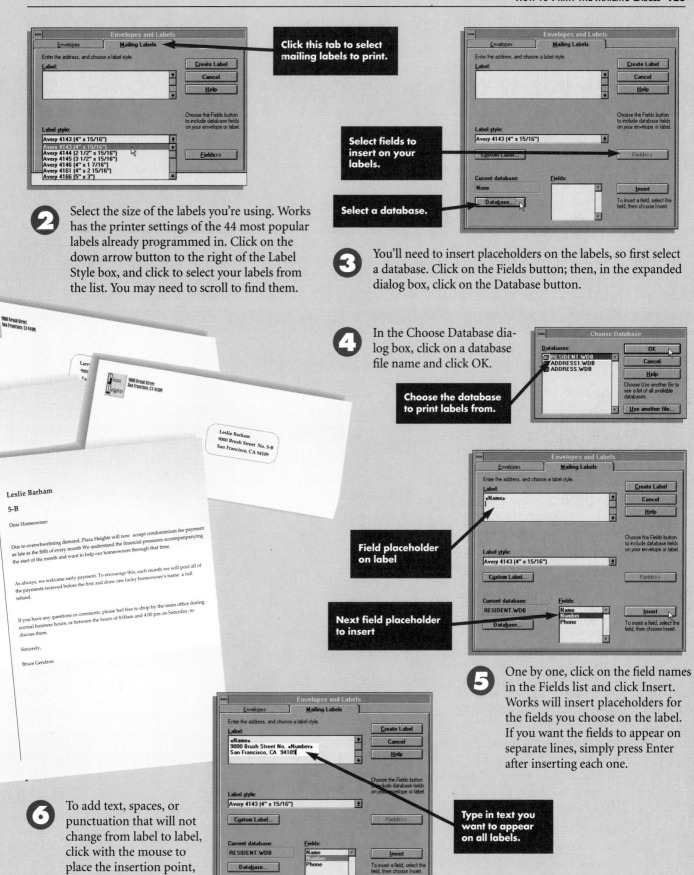

Click this tab to select mailing labels to print.

Select fields to insert on your labels.

Select a database.

2 Select the size of the labels you're using. Works has the printer settings of the 44 most popular labels already programmed in. Click on the down arrow button to the right of the Label Style box, and click to select your labels from the list. You may need to scroll to find them.

3 You'll need to insert placeholders on the labels, so first select a database. Click on the Fields button; then, in the expanded dialog box, click on the Database button.

4 In the Choose Database dialog box, click on a database file name and click OK.

Choose the database to print labels from.

Field placeholder on label

Next field placeholder to insert

5 One by one, click on the field names in the Fields list and click Insert. Works will insert placeholders for the fields you choose on the label. If you want the fields to appear on separate lines, simply press Enter after inserting each one.

6 To add text, spaces, or punctuation that will not change from label to label, click with the mouse to place the insertion point, and simply type it in.

Type in text you want to appear on all labels.

CHAPTER 14

Combining the Features of Microsoft Works

By now you've seen how powerful the individual parts of Microsoft Works are. The Word processor, spreadsheet, and database programs give you the resources to automate many diverse and complex tasks. Using these programs individually, however, applies only a fraction of the power of Works.

In the first 12 chapters of this book you learned about the three most-used parts of Works. In Chapter 13, you touched on new ground when you learned how to merge word processor documents with databases. This chapter is devoted to exploring this new realm: combining information from the various programs in Works.

How to Combine Objects by Using the Clipboard

You've used the Windows clipboard to copy text and spreadsheet information from one location and paste it in another location within a document. What you may not know is that you can also apply these techniques to copy blocks of information, or *objects*, from one type of document to another.

For example, you may want to place a table from your quarterly budget spreadsheet in the memo you're drafting on the word processor. You might instead want to copy a table of outstanding balances from a spreadsheet to your customer information database, and then merge that data with a bill you've set up with the word processor. While the possibilities of objects to copy and paste are endless, the techniques stay the same.

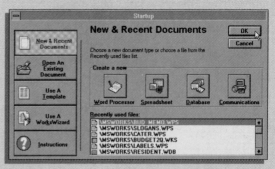

1 To speed data transfer, start by opening both of the documents you want to work with: the document containing the object you want to copy, and the document in which you want to paste the object.

TIP SHEET

▶ The Windows clipboard can transfer objects, not only within Works, but between programs as well. You can copy objects in other programs and paste them into Works. You can also copy objects in Works and paste them into other programs.

▶ When you're working with more than one Works document open at a time, use the Ctrl+Tab key combination to switch between them rapidly.

6 Open the Edit menu and click Paste. Works will place the copied object in the location you selected.

Select the source document.

2 Click on the Window menu to open it, and look at the file names at its bottom. You should see the names of both of the files you just opened. Click on the name of the file containing the object you want to copy. Works will switch to that document.

Drag to select.

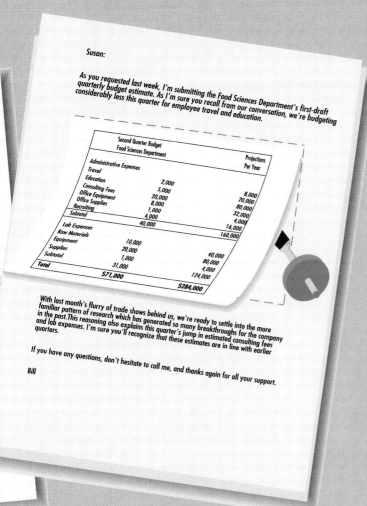

3 Locate the object you want to copy, and select it using the standard click-and-drag technique. Open the Edit menu and click on Copy.

Paste

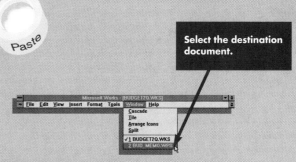

Select the destination document.

4 Open the Window menu again, but this time click on the destination document to switch to it.

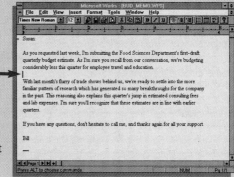

Insertion point

5 Click with the mouse in the destination document to either activate the cell or place the insertion point at the location you want to paste.

How to Use the Insert Commands

Using the Insert commands, you can place a wide variety of objects in your word processor documents. These objects can originate in other parts of Works or in entirely different programs. The Insert commands work somewhat like the clipboard with one major exception: Rather than copy an existing object from an open application, you open an application to create an object of the type you specify.

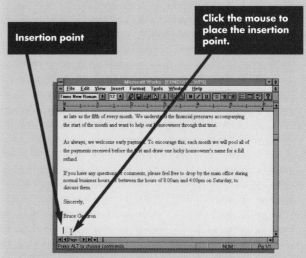

Insertion point

Click the mouse to place the insertion point.

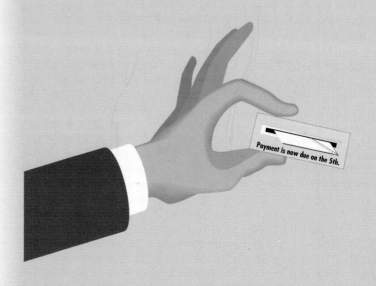

▶ **1** Click in your document at the location you want to insert an object.

Payment is now due on the 5th.

TIP SHEET

▶ **The object types available in the Insert Object dialog box depend on the applications you have installed on your computer. For example, if you have Microsoft Excel installed, you will be able to select Excel Chart, Worksheet, and Macrosheet objects.**

▶ **The Insert menu contains shortcuts for inserting several kinds of objects. Select from these menu items to skip the Insert Object dialog box.**

▶ **The Insert commands, along with the general nature of the word processor, make the word processor the best place to assemble documents from objects of different types.**

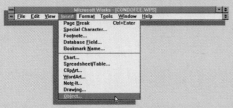

2 Click on the Insert menu to open it, and click again on Object.

3 In the Insert Object dialog box, click to make a selection from the Object Type list. You may need to scroll the list to find the object type you want. When you are through, click the OK button.

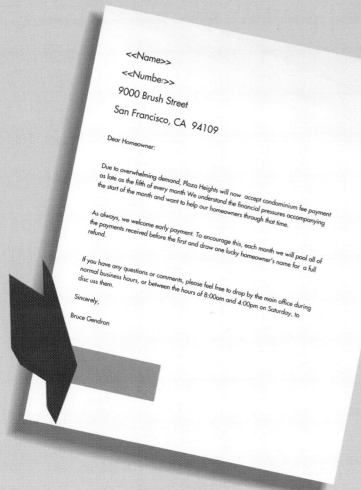

4 The window you see next will vary widely depending on the object type you choose. The Microsoft Note-It window allows you to select an image, add a caption, and optionally add a pop-up message that will appear if a user double-clicks on the image in your document. Create or complete the object you want to insert, and click the OK button if it is available. If you do not see an OK button, select Update from the File menu of the open object window. Works will place the object in your document.

CHAPTER 15

Connecting with Other Computers

Communication can be described as the exchange of information. You've long understood the value of communication between people, but you may wonder how you can benefit from communication between computers. The answer is simple. You probably store much of the information you use every day in your computer, and the same is true for millions of other people. When your computer can communicate directly with other computers, you have easier and more-direct access to all that information.

The possible sources of information are limitless: E-mail can connect you quickly and inexpensively to friends and associates all over the world. You might have a special interest like beer brewing or whale watching and want to exchange ideas through a computer forum. You could take advantage of an unbelievable range of public domain data files ranging from recent space photographs to press releases from the White House. Maybe you're in the Bahamas and want to send a file to your boss at work so she'll think you're working at home.

Hitchhiking on the information superhighway is discouraged, so you'll need to gather a few things before you can travel there: First, you'll need an access road—any but the noisiest telephone line will work. Next, you'll need a vehicle. You already have a computer, but you'll also need a *modem*, a small device for connecting your computer to a telephone line. Finally, to go in style, you'll need a driver. This is where Microsoft Works becomes your best friend.

How to Set Up Your Modem in Microsoft Works

Before you begin your travels, you'll need to get your affairs in order. Just like you had to set up Works when you got it, you'll need to take a few steps to ensure that Works, your modem, and all of the other parts of your computer are ready to work together.

1 If you have an external modem, first make sure that it is connected to both your computer and the telephone line, and check that it is plugged in and turned on. If you have an internal modem, check that it is connected to the telephone line, and in the case of some notebook computers, that it is inserted properly and turned on.

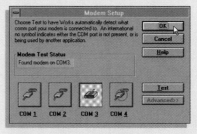

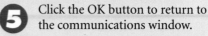

5 Click the OK button to return to the communications window.

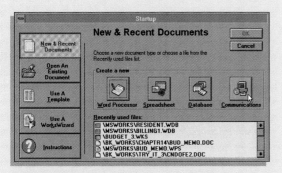

2 Start Works. In the Startup dialog box, click on the square Communications button to begin a new communications session.

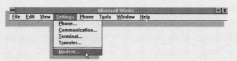

3 The first time you run the communications program, Works will display the Modem Setup dialog box. If you see the Easy Connect dialog box instead, click the Cancel button. Next select Modem from the Settings menu. Works will then display the Modem Setup dialog box.

4 Your modem is connected to your computer through a data channel called *COM port.* ("COM" is short for "communication.") This port may be an external connector on the back of your computer, or it may be an internal card. Works needs to know where your modem is located, so click on the Test button. Works will scan your COM ports for a modem and automatically select the correct one for you.

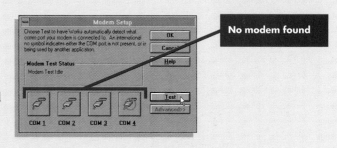

How to Change Communication Settings

When you talk to another person, you generally know ahead of time what language you will speak and what rules of grammar you will use. Unfortunately, when you set up your computer to "talk" to another computer, you generally can't assume what *protocols*, or rules of communication, the other computer will be set up to use.

This means a little legwork on your part. Before you dial with your modem, you'll need to find someone familiar with the other computer (the one you want to communicate with) and ask a few questions about protocols. Once you know what protocols the other computer is using, you'll want to change your Microsoft Works communication settings to use the same ones.

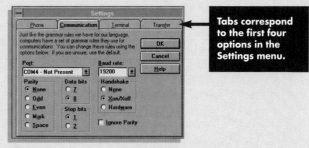

1 Open the Settings menu and click on Communication. Works will respond by opening the Settings dialog box. Note the four tabs at the top of the dialog box. They correspond to the first four options in the Settings menu.

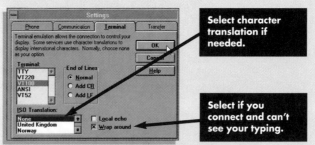

8 If you'll be connecting to a computer that uses a foreign language, select the country from the ISO Translation list box (select None for the United States). This setting lets Works know how to handle special foreign characters. When you are finished making selections from the Settings dialog box, click on the OK button.

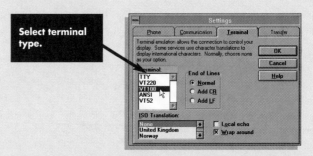

7 You may need to find out ahead of time what terminal types are supported by the computer you're connecting to. Often, however, many different types are available, and you can select one for Works to emulate after you connect.

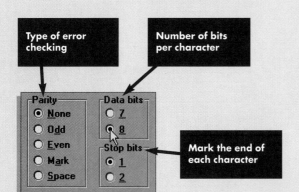

Type of error checking

Number of bits per character

Mark the end of each character

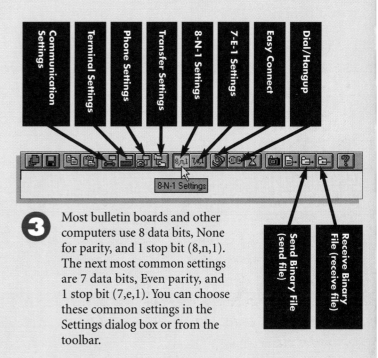

2 The most important options in this dialog box are Data Bits, Parity, and Stop Bits. These settings describe how to interpret the stream of data bits, or ones and zeros, traveling between computers. The Data Bits setting is the number of bits in each character that you send and receive. The Parity setting describes how your computer will check each character for accuracy. The Stop Bits setting tells how to mark the end of each character. Before you can connect computers, you must match the settings the other computer will use.

3 Most bulletin boards and other computers use 8 data bits, None for parity, and 1 stop bit (8,n,1). The next most common settings are 7 data bits, Even parity, and 1 stop bit (7,e,1). You can choose these common settings in the Settings dialog box or from the toolbar.

Send Binary File (send file)

Receive Binary File (receive file)

4 Check the Port setting to ensure that it is the same port Works found in the Modem Setup dialog box. If it isn't, select the correct one in the Port drop-down list box.

Do you speak my language ?

¿ Habla mi idioma ?

5 You'll need to select a *baud rate*. This is the speed, in bits per second, at which data will travel between computers (higher numbers mean faster communication). Select the fastest setting that your modem will support (it's in the modem documentation). Don't worry that the other computer's modem might be faster or slower. They'll "negotiate" to find the fastest speed that they both support.

6 Some computers will respond directly to your keystrokes and control the display of text on your monitor. If you will be connecting to one of these, you'll need to check your terminal settings. Click on the Terminal tab at the top of the Settings dialog box, or select Terminal from the Settings menu.

How to Connect to Another Computer

Once you know and establish the communications settings, you can connect to a wide assortment of computer services. The example here connects to Microsoft Download Service. This service is a computer bulletin board that lets you download files (transfer them from a large central computer to yours) for updating Microsoft products that you already license or own. The communication settings for the service are 8,n,1; and it supports baud rates of 1,200; 2,400; 9,600; and 14,400 bits per second.

The example on this page includes a telephone call to Washington State. If you want to follow along with the example, you may want to look over this and the next spread first, so that you don't spend unnecessary time on a long-distance call.

TIP SHEET

▶ **Works ignores the hyphens you put in telephone numbers. If you need a short pause between numbers while dialing a telephone number, add a comma where you want the pause. If you need a longer pause, add more than one comma.**

▶ **To save all your settings in a file, so you don't have to reenter them the next time you connect, select Save from the File menu. Later, you can reuse them by opening the file you saved, or you can select the service by name from the Easy Connect dialog box.**

▶ **Some computer services have on-line charges. That means they charge you for the time you spend connected to them. Always ask if you will be billed before you make a connection. (Microsoft Download Service does not have an on-line charge.)**

▶ **1** Double-check that the settings you chose in the previous two spreads are correct. Then, open the Settings menu and click on Phone. The Settings dialog box will open to the Phone page.

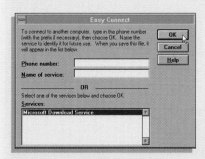

8 In later sessions, you'll see the Easy Connect dialog box when you start the Works communication program. To open it at any time other than start-up, select Easy Connect in the Phone menu. To reconnect to a service, simply select it from the Services list and click OK. Click OK again when Works asks you if you want to connect to the other computer.

2 Type in the telephone number of the computer you want to call. Next type in a descriptive name for the service. This name will appear in the Easy Connect dialog box the next time you start the communications program.

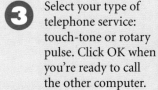

Telephone number of other computer

This name will appear in the Easy Connect dialog box.

3 Select your type of telephone service: touch-tone or rotary pulse. Click OK when you're ready to call the other computer.

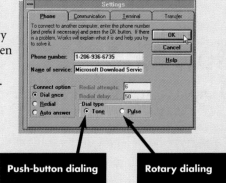

Push-button dialing   **Rotary dialing**

4 To dial the number you entered in step 2 and establish a connection with the other computer, select Dial from the Phone menu.

Ring !!!

Ring !!!

Type the letter that appears in square brackets to issue a command.

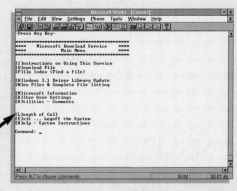

5 Every information service offers different features, but many computer bulletin boards have a look and feel similar to the Microsoft Download Service. The first time you connect, the service will ask you for your name and location. It then greets you, shows service news summaries, and shows you to its Main menu.

6 To execute a command in any menu, type the letter that appears in square brackets. You don't need to press Enter afterward. For example, to find out how long you've been connected, press L on your keyboard. (Downloading files is covered in the next spread.)

7 When you're finished with your business, follow the instructions on the screen to return to the Main menu, and press E to exit.

How to Send and Receive Files

Transferring files is a highly specialized form of communicating with another computer. Because of this, many transfer protocols, or languages, have evolved for doing nothing but transferring files. Four of the best transfer protocols are provided for your use in Microsoft Works.

TIP SHEET

▶ **Sending a file to another computer is much the same as receiving one. Instead of selecting Receive File from the Tools menu, however, select Send File. You'll need to locate the file for Works to send. It's a good idea to know where it is before you connect to the other computer. If possible, put it in the same folder as Works for easy access.**

▶ **If you know what transfer protocol you will be using for your transfer, save money by selecting it before you connect to the other computer.**

▶ **The four transfer protocols all have unique characteristics. XMODEM is the most commonly used, and is quite reliable for transferring data accurately. YMODEM is faster than XMODEM, but does not work well with a noisy telephone line. ZMODEM is faster than YMODEM and as reliable as XMODEM, but is not quite as commonly used. Use it when you can. Kermit, the slowest of the four, is also the most reliable, working well with noisy telephone lines. Use it only when necessary.**

▶ **The example here downloads REVERS.EXE. Using File Manager, copy this file to your Windows directory and then double-click on it. It will expand into REVERSI.EXE and three supporting files. REVERSI.EXE is a game that shipped with Windows 3.0. You can double-click on it in File Manager to run it, or you can create a program item in Program Manager and run it from there. See your Windows 3.1 documentation for more help.**

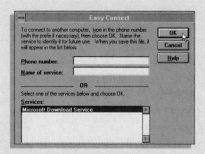

▶ **1** Following the procedures explained earlier in this chapter, connect Works to another computer that will let you receive, or download, a file.

Options appear when the download is completed.

8 Wait for an indicator that the transfer is complete. Once you see it, you are free to interact with the other computer exactly as you did before the transfer.

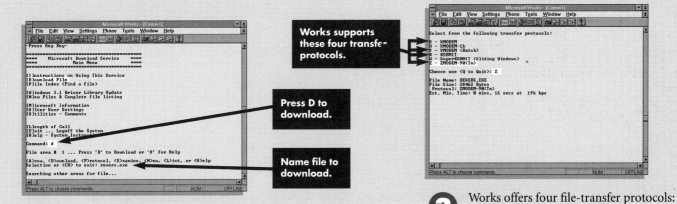

Works supports these four transfer protocols.

Press D to download.

Name file to download.

2 Send the other computer the signal that you want to download a file. (In this case, press D.) Once you tell it the file you want (in this case, REVERS.EXE), the other computer will ask you what transfer protocol to use.

3 Works offers four file-transfer protocols: XMODEM, YMODEM, ZMODEM, and Kermit. Select one of them.

Connect

4 The other computer will tell you to initiate the download in your communications software.

5 Select Transfer from the Settings menu and select the same transfer protocol as you did in step 3. Then click the OK button.

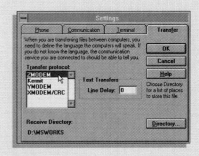

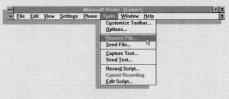

7 Many services will indicate how much of the file you have received and how much you have left. Microsoft Download Service tells you how many bytes and what percentage of the file you have received.

6 To begin the transfer, select Receive File from the Tools menu. By default, the file will go into the Works folder.

TRY IT!

With your new database and object transferring skills still fresh in your mind, it's time to give them a short workout to bring them to peak condition. Follow these steps to gather information from a variety of sources, create this database and billing statement, and then merge the two. Many of the steps include a chapter reference in case you would like additional information.

1

Start Works and open a new database document by clicking on the square Database button in the Startup dialog box. *Chapter 12*

Type in the title of your form at the top of the screen. *Chapter 12*

Click on the form where you want to insert the first field, and then select Field from the Insert menu. *Chapter 12*

Type the name of the field, Customer Name, into the Insert Field dialog box and click on OK. *Chapter 12*

Repeat steps 3 and 4 for the Address and Balance fields.

Drag the field names to align the colons vertically, and then drag the handles on the right side of the field lines to lengthen them uniformly. *Chapter 12*

Click on the List View button to switch the database to List view. *Chapter 12*

Enter into the database the information shown in the illustration. When you are through, double-click on the field names at the tops of the columns to resize the column widths. *Chapter 12*

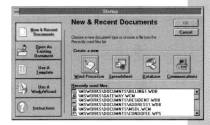

Save the database with the Save command in the File menu, but don't close it yet.

Select Create New File in the File menu to show the Startup dialog box. Click on the square Word Processor button to create a new document. *Chapter 4*

Type in the text from the illustration. *Chapter 4*

Continue to next page ►

TRY IT!

Continue
below

14

Back in the
Insert Field
dialog box,
click on the
Customer
Name field
and then the
Insert but-
ton. Works will replace the selected text
with a field placeholder, and the Cancel
button will change to Close. Click on
the Close button to return to the document. *Chapter 13*

15

Repeat steps
12 and 14 to
replace *ad-
dress 1, ad-
dress 2,* and
xxx (the ac-
count bal-
ance) with the appropriate fields from
the open database. When you are finished, save but don't close the word
processor document. *Chapter 4*

12

Select the text
"customer name" at
the top of the docu-
ment, and then click
on the Database Field command in
the Insert menu. *Chapter 13*

13

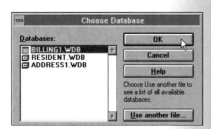

In the Insert
Field dialog
box, click on
the Database
button. In
the Choose Database dialog box that
opens next, your open database file
should appear at the top of the list.
Click on it, and click on the OK button. *Chapter 13*

16

Click on the Startup Dialog button to display the Startup dialog box. Click on the
square Spreadsheet button to create a
new spreadsheet document. *Chapter 8*

17

Type in the text and numbers shown in the illustration. For cell F6, enter the contents of the formula bar, and then copy that formula to the three cells below it. Remember both that you can select a block of cells to speed up data entry, and that you can double-click on the column labels to adjust their width to fit the data within them. *Chapters 9–11*

18

When you have completed the spreadsheet, save it, but don't close it. *Chapter 8*

19

Next, transfer the account balances from the spreadsheet where they are calculated, to the database where they can merge with the word-processed billing statement. Click and drag to select cells F6:F9, the numbers representing new balances, and then select Copy from the Edit menu. *Chapter 10*

20

Click on the Window menu to pull it down, and select the name of the database file you saved in step 9. *Chapter 14*

21

In the database document, click in the top row of the Account Balance column, select Edit from the menu bar, and then select Paste. Works will paste the balance numbers from the spreadsheet into the database where they can next merge with the billing statement. *Chapter 14*

22

Click on the Window menu again, but this time switch to the word processor file you saved in step 15 by selecting it from the menu. *Chapter 14*

23

Get set to print the word processor file by selecting Print from the File menu. *Chapter 13*

24

In the Print dialog box, confirm that the Print Merge check box is checked and click on OK.

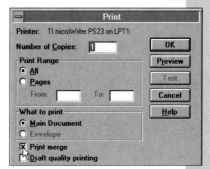

Select your open database in the Choose Database dialog box, and then click on OK again. Works will merge the database fields into your word processor document, including the up-to-date account balances you calculated in the spreadsheet. *Chapter 13*

INDEX

A

Accessories document window, 13

Accessories program group, 8–9

Active cell, 72–73
  in spreadsheet document, 69, 86

ADJUST pointer, changing column width with, 114

alignment buttons, on toolbar, 18

Alignment dialog box, 98–99

Alt key, issuing commands with, 12–13

application window, 8, 19

arrow keys
  navigating through documents, 40–41
  navigating in spreadsheets, 86–87
  positioning cursor in dialog boxes, 14
  scrolling window contents, 13

Automatic Word Selection check box, in Options dialog box, 36

Autosum button, 82

AVG function, 82

B

Backspace (←) key
  correcting typos, 24
  deleting spreadsheet cell information, 92–93
  deleting text, 14, 39

backup copies, creating and saving, 30, 76

baud rate, setting, 135

Between Lines text box, in Paragraph dialog box, 54–55

Bold button, on toolbar, 18

boldface, formatting, 45–47

Breaks and Spacing tab, 55

bulletin board, connecting to, 136–137

C

calculations, in spreadsheet documents, 80–81

Calculator, 8

Cancel button, 14, 70

Caps Lock key, 24

cell address, 86

cell reference box
  erasing information from, 71
  in spreadsheet document, 69, 70

cells
  aligning information in, 98–99
  copying, 90–91
  entering information into, 70–71
  moving contents of, 88–89
  removing information from, 92–93
  selecting, 72–73
  in spreadsheet documents, 68–69

check box, 15

Choose Database dialog box, 119

clearing information from spreadsheet cells, 92–93

clicking the mouse, 11

Clipboard. *See* Windows Clipboard

closing documents, 27

closing windows, 13

column labels, in spreadsheet documents, 69

column width, 98, 112, 114

comma format, for numbers, 97

communications, 1–3

Communications button, in Startup dialog box, 133

communications settings, changing, 134–135

COM port, 133

connecting to another computer, 136–137

Control Menu boxes, 8–9, 19, 27, 69

Copy button, 18

copying
  cells in spreadsheets, 90–91
  from one document type to another, 126–127

COUNT function, 82

"Create a new" button group, in Startup dialog box, 23, 69

Ctrl key, 12–13, 41

Ctrl+End
  moving to bottom of window contents, 12
  moving to end of spreadsheet, 86

Ctrl+S (Save), 76

Ctrl+Z (Undo), 39

Cue Cards, 19, 32

Currency format, for numbers, 97

Current Database box, in Insert Field dialog box, 119

Custom Labels dialog box, 122

Custom Labels tab, in Envelopes and Labels dialog box, 122

custom menu, 6

cut and paste
  moving spreadsheet cell contents with, 88–89
  moving text with, 42–43

Cut button, 18